SEATTLE

TOWNSCAPE

WALKS

on
Route 19

a real
VW
bug

caught
by a Troll

210 miles
connected by
52 maps for
52 weeks of
adventure.

a real
statue
of
Lenin
from
Russia

a real rocket

by
Tyler Burgess

*Author and
Illustrator*

On Route 36

A tribute to the heroes of the
Civil War in the Grand Army of
the Republic Cemetery.

Published by:
Walk With Me
1430 Williamette St. #579
Eugene, OR 97401

Printed in Canada

These are unique routes I
designed as I walked them.
As we all know, shift happens.
Construction changes and
business turnovers alter the
areas. Updates are welcome.

original
cobble
stones

Mileage is by gmap-pedometer.om.
Used by permission.
Base maps are Seattle iMAP
and City of Winslow, used by
permission.

Other books written and
illustrated by Tyler Burgess.

"Walking Made Powerful"
"Eugene, Oregon Walks"
"Oregon Townscape Walks"

ISBN 978-0-9816599-2-3

Dedication

To my wonderful children,
Damon Cole, Sara Cole and her wonderful
husband, Bill Barnes.

Thank you to each of them for
the many walks and talks
that naturally go with the
experience. We have walked
Seattle for many years, as they
live there, and I in Eugene, Oregon.

Now I can also enjoy Seattle
walks with my grandchildren,
Theo and Rosie, when I visit.
A big thank you to their
parents for cultivating a love
of walking and exploring in
my grandchildren. Because,
that is what we do!

BEST in SEATTLE

After considerable research,
my son Damon recommends.

<u>Coffee:</u> Victrola Coffee
411 15 Av. E
<u>Bagels:</u> Bagel Deli
340 15 Av. E
<u>Pizza:</u> Palmero Pizza
350 15 Av. E

All are on # 36 Grand Army of the Republic.
We designed this walk together.

Location of Routes

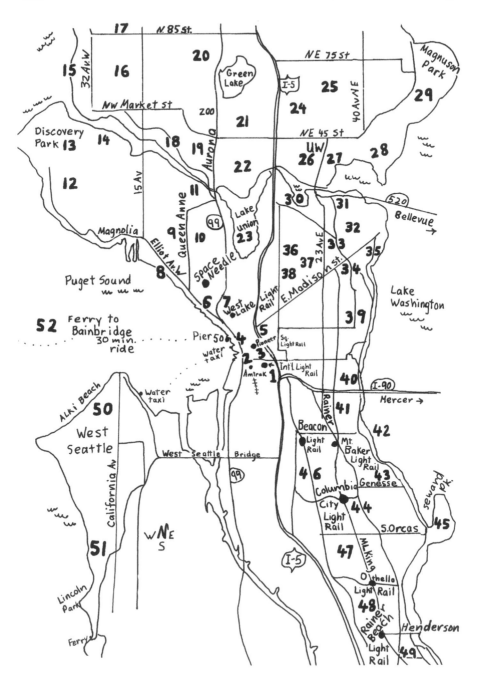

Table of Contents

1

Start and Connecting Points

Start Point	Route	Maximum Miles	Connects to
Arboretum Playfield	33. Above the Arboretum	3.3	# 37
Arboretum Playfield	32. Arboretum	2.0	# 31
Arboretum Playfield	34. Arboretum to Madison Peak	3.5	# 35, 39
Ballard Locks	16. Best of Ballard	6.4	# 17, 15
Ballard Locks	15. Golden Garden Park	4.75	# 16
Ballard Locks	14. Locks to Discovery Park	3.7	# 13
Beacon Hill Light Rail	46. Beacon Hill	4.7	# 41, 47
Burke-Gilman Park	29. B-G Park to Magnuson Park	6.1	# 28
Columbia City Light Rail	45. Columbia City to Seward Park	7.5	# 43
Columbia City Light Rail	44. Historic Columbia City	1.0	# 45
Discovery Park	13. Historic Grounds, Trail	4.3	# 12, 14
Ferry Terminal	52. Bainbridge Island	4.1	# 2, 4, 41
Fremont	18. Fremont and Ballard Bridge	4.2	# 11, 16, 19, 23
Fremont	19. Fremont to Woodland Park	5.5	# 11, 18, 20, 23
Fremont, south of	11. Queen Anne North	2.5	# 9, 10, 18, 19, 23
Genesse Park	43. Genesse Park to Mt. Baker	4.4	# 40, 45
Green Lake	20. Green Lake to Greenwood	5.0	# 19
Green Lake	24. Green Lake to UW Campus	4.1	# 25, 26, 27
Green Lake	21. Green Lake to Wallingford	5.0	# 22
Int'l. District Light Rail	1. International District	2.3	# 3, 41
Int'l. District Light Rail	2. Int'l. Dist. to Pike Market	2.5	# 41
Laurelhurst	28. Laurelhurst	5.8	# 27, 29
Madison Park	35. Madison Park	4.5	# 34, 39
Magnolia Park	12. Magnolia to Discovery Park	6.8	# 13
Montlake Comm. Ctr.	23. Lake Union Loop	6.3	# 10, 11, 18, 19, 22
Montlake Comm. Ctr.	31. Montlake to Foster Island	4.0	# 27, 32, 33
Montlake Comm. Ctr.	30. Portage Bay Loop	3.2	# 23, 26, 27
Mt. Baker Light Rail	41. Lake Wash. to Puget Sound	5.6	# 40, 43, 46
Mt. Baker Light Rail	42. Mt. Baker-Light Rail to Beach	2.0	# 40, 43
Mt. Baker Light Rail	40. Mt. Baker to Leschi	5.1	# 39, 43
NW 85 and 23 Av. NW	17. Christmas Lights	2.1	# 16
Othello Light Rail	47. Chief Sealth Trail A	4.0	# 46, 48
Othello Light Rail	48. Chief Sealth Trail B	2.8	# 47, 48
Pike Place Market	6. Pike Mkt. to Olympic Sculpture	2.3	# 7, 8
Pike Place Market	5. Pike Mkt. to Historic Homes	2.5	# 38
Pioneer Sq. Light Rail	4. Pioneer Sq. to Pike Market	2.2	# 3, 5, 6, 41
Pioneer Sq. Light Rail	3. Pioneer Square	1.3	# 1, 2, 41
Powell-Barnett Park	39. Leschi to Madrona	3.75	# 34, 35, 40
Rainer Beach Light Rail	49. Chief Sealth Trail C	2.7	# 48
Ravenna NW and Park Rd.	25. Candy Cane Lane	.2	# 24
Space Needle	9. Queen Anne West	6.0	# 10, 11, 23
Space Needle	8. Space Needle to Elliot Bay	3.5	# 6
Space Needle	7. Space Needle to Pike Mkt.	2.7	# 2, 4, 5, 21
UW Central Plaza	26. UW and the Ave.	2.0	# 23, 24, 30
UW Central Plaza	27. UW Natural Area	4.0	# 24, 28, 30
Volunteer Park	37. Capitol Hill	4.0	# 33
Volunteer Park	36. Grand Army of Republic	4.0	# 23
Volunteer Park	38. Harvard-Belmont Historic	4.0	# 5
Wallingford Park	22. Wallingford to Gas Works	3.0	# 21, 23
West Seattle	50. West Seattle Beach	13.6	# 51
West Seattle	51. Lincoln Park to Downtown	8.6	# 50

Legend

● Start and finish here. **R** turn Right.

••• shorter option

– – – trail **L** turn Left

⁖⁖ hill

mi. Mileage **P** parking

Food: May be a cafe, deli, grocery store, coffee shop or restaurant. If you want to use their restroom, please purchase something.

RR: Public restrooms. The city has just cut the number of days they are open.

38 Large numbers on maps indicate a connection to another route number.

on Columbia city to Seward Park Route 44

Lodging *Distance from Amtrak station*

Downtown

1. Best Western Pioneer Square
.4 mile from Amtrak
77 Yesler Way, 206-340-1234

2. Hotel 1000, Luxury.
.6 mile to Amtrak
1000 First Av. 877-315-1088

3. •Green Tortoise, Hostel
1 mile from Amtrak
105 Pike St. at First Av. 206-340-1222

4. Moore Hotel, Budget
1.2 mile from Amtrak
1926 Second Av. 206-448-4852

Near Seattle Center, Space Needle

5. •Inn at Queen Anne, Budget
2.4 mile from Amtrak
505 First Av. N 206-282-7359

6. •Mar Queen, Botique hotel
2.6 mile from Amtrak
600 Queen Anne Av. N. 206-282-7407

Introduction

"Seattle Townscape Walks" is a Sasumi
 210 mile love letter
celebrating:
> •charming neighborhoods and parks,
> • spectacular natural setting,
> • fabulous urban design,
> • friendly folks.

Savor the beauty with each step.
Linger at Gucci's window,
Browse a trendy botique.
Sketch a historic home.

Gawk at breath-taking views:
 • Olympic Mountains
 • North Cascade Mountains
 • Mt. Rainer

Pause to peruse fascinating
history plaques punctuating
buildings, parks,
benches and fences.

Propel by pedestrian power
•52 walks for
 • 52 weeks for 210 miles a year.

It is like walking from
adventure to adventure.
drawing you into the magic
that is Seattle.

What is a Townscape Walk?

"For a city is a dramatic event in the environment." George Cullen, "Townscapes" 1961

A townscape walk presents Seattle as a dramatic event. I join together existing structures into a pattern to experience the warmth, power and vitality of Seattle. You are drawn through cozy neighborhoods and the small towns creating a city,

Thus experiencing a sense of the people and place, not an impersonal city. Versus wandering or strict lines that make it appear dull, lifeless, confusing or difficult. A spectacular front porch view greets you instead of a side view.

School yard art

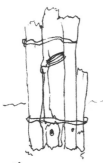

Mt. Rainer peaks over the Chief Sealth Trail A, as a dramatic view takes your breath away upon descent, instead being obscured by buildings and trees.

What makes a walk dramatic? Look for the following features on the unique routes I designed.

Library

7

"The Line of Life" Why is this city here? Walks start at the early settlements along the harbor, on to downtown and early neighborhoods and small towns that became Seattle. Read the many history plaques. Drop in to the museums.

one ton Gold Bars
Klondike Museum

"Grandiose Vista" "It links you, in the foreground, to the remote landscape. Thus producing a sense of power or omnipresence." Or, as expressed by Dr. Suess, "I'm Yertle the Turtle! Oh, Marvelous Me! For I am ruler of all that I see!"

view of MT. Rainier

"The Mystery of the Emerging View" What is around the corner, over the hill, down the path? Do we go up that steep hill? No, I did not want to, either. You turn at the bottom of the hill for a more gradual ascent. Most ascents are in the first part. Descents can be steep. Reverse the direction, if you dare.

Handling the hills!

Silhouette: With a curve, a filigree, a steeple, the building soars up, but also catches the sky and brings it down to the building, Netting the sky as a butterfly net catches a butterfly.

8

"SEEING IN DETAIL": a window, symbol, arch
a column, sculptures, garden art

Bridges: functional art, beauty, individuality
create drama. Where will it take me?

Outdoor rooms: Porches, gazebos, benches.
Creation of special places of
enclosure, seclusion. Does it
invite social activity?

Fences: Is it functional, a work of art?
How many types and kinds do you see?

Architectural Styles: Create nostalgia, drama,
give character and personality.

Gardens: abound in Seattle, creating earthy
connection amidst the concrete.

Trees: Are they an architectural feature lining
a path or street, creating a sense of
enclosure around a building, or a
natural stand, "pleased to dwell among us."

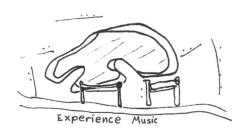

Experience Music

All quotes are from "Townscapes"
by George Cullen, 1961.

A Walk for Every Occasion

Challenge: 52 walks for 52 weeks in a year.

Date Walks: Walk, eat, walk, eat, walk
 See maps for FooD stops.

Kid Walks: Park to Park, # 29, 43
 Mt. Baker Light Rail to Beach, #42
 Park to Palermo Pizza, #36

Christmas Walks: Candy Cane Lane #25
 Christmas Lights #17

Spring Tree Blossoms:
 early-March: Montlake to Foster Island, on
 Royal Court #31
 UW Natural Area, #27
 mid-March: Chief Sealth A, C, #47, 49
 Arboretum, #32

Walk Over Water: Locks in Ballard, #14, 16
 Fremont, Ballard Bridges #18
 Lake Union, #23
 Portage Bay Loop, #30, #31

Rememberance Walks in Natural Areas:
 #15, 27, 32, 45, 50

Longer Distances:
 • Connect walks with a common
 start.
 • All routes connect to another.
 The big numbers on maps
 indicate a connect point.

10

International District

Distance: 1.8 mi. or 2.3 miles. 255 ft. elevation
Start/finish: International/Chinatown Light Rail
Exit to Jackson st. go **L**.
L on 2nd Av. S.
Into Qwest parking lot. veer
L to stairs. Cross bridge.
Cross 4th, go ½ block.
R through courtyard. **L** at end.
L on 6th.

Kobe Park

Cross Main, go **R** ½ block.
L up to Danny Woo Gardens.
Veer **R** on main path to top.
Pick any path back down.
L on Main, ½ block.
R on Maynard. **L** on Lane, 1 block.
L on 7th. (for 1.8 mi., **L** on Jackson.)
R on King. **L** on 12th, 1 block.
Cross Jackson, go **L** to 5th.

Directions to start:
By car: <u>From I-5 south</u>, Exit 164B.
R on 4th Av. S. First **R** on Brougham.
R at end. Parking under bridge.
OR **R** on Jackson. **R** on 2nd
in to Quest parking lot.

<u>From I-5 north</u> Exit 165B
on to Union. **L** at 5th Av. N.
R on Madison to end.
Parking under bridge.
OR from Madison, **L** on 2nd
to Quest parking lot.
Join walk enroute.

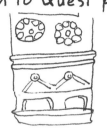

Bus. from Downtown, 143 to 2 Av. S and S. Jackson.
11 **Light rail:** International District

1

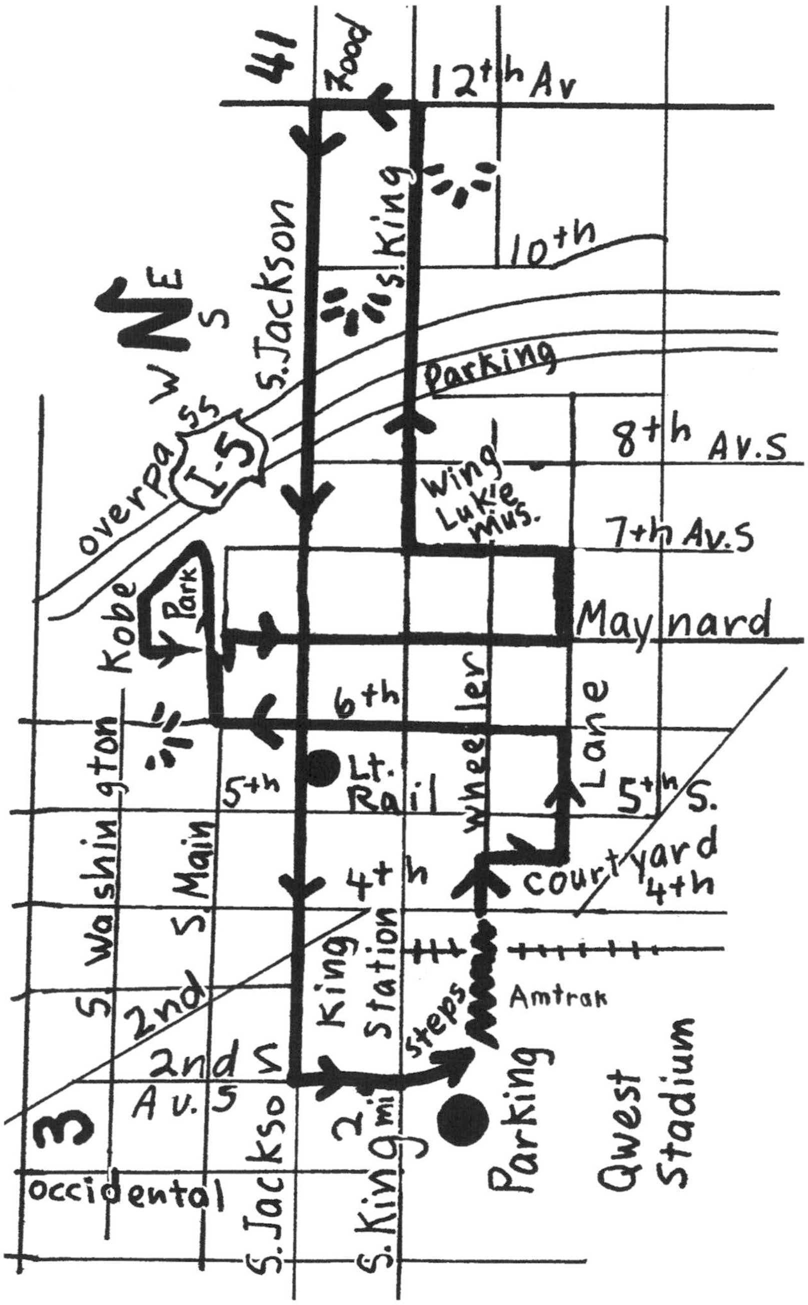
41
Food
12th Av
S. King
S. Jackson
10th
N
W
E
S
overpass
I-5
Parking
8th Av. S
Wing Luke Mus.
7th Av. S
Kobe Park
Maynard
6th
Lt. Rail
5th
Wheeler
Lane
5th S.
courtyard
4th
S. Washington
S. Main
4th
King Station
steps
Amtrak
2nd
2nd Av. S
3
Parking
Qwest Stadium
S. Jackso
2 mi
occidental
S. Jackson
S. King

Int'l. District to Pike Market

Distance: <u>1.2 mi.</u> to WestLake Light Rail. Flat.
2.5 mi., 77 ft. elevation

Start/finish:-<u>Int'l. District Light Rail</u> or <u>Bus</u>
(Exit to Jackson St. Go **L**.)
-<u>King Station, Amtrak Train</u>
(Straight on King St., 1 block.)
Restrooms at Pike Market.

R on 2 Av.S. Curves **L** into 2 Av.
(for 1.2 mi. **R** on Pine st. one block
to WestLake Center for
Light Rail or Monorail to the
Seattle Conv.Center, at Space
Needle.)

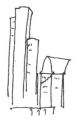

Seattle
Art
Museum
at
2 Av. +
Univers.

L on Pike St. into Market.
Explore. Exit Market
past the flower stalls.
L on Virginia st. to Park
for view.
Downhill on Western Av.
R in elevator to Waterfront.
OR continue to Pike Hill Climb.
R down steps to harbor.
L along water front.

R up stairs at Marion st., go **L**
Over the bridge above streets.
Cross 1 Ave. Go **R**.
L on S. Jackson to Light Rail, BUS.
OR **L** on King to King Station,
Amtrak train.

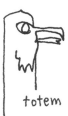

totem

Directions to start:

By car: <u>From I-5 south</u>, Exit 164B.
R on 4th Av.S. First **R** on Brougham.
R at end. Parking under bridge.
OR **R** on Jackson. **R** on 2nd
in to Quest parking lot.

<u>From I-5 north</u> Exit 165B
on to Union. **L** at 5th Av. N.
R on Madison to end.
Parking under bridge.
OR from Madison, **L** on 2nd
to Quest parking lot.
Join walk enroute.

Bus. from Downtown, 143 to 2 Av. S and S. Jackson.
Light rail: International District

Pioneer Square

Distance: 1.3 miles. 64 ft. elevation gain.

Start/finish: Pioneer Square Light Rail
at James St. and 3rd Ave.

Walk downhill on James St.
L on 1st Ave. S.
L on King, one block.
L on Occidental Av. S.

old cable
car stop
shelter

R on Yesler Way, one block.
R on 2nd Ext. Av. S, one block.
R around the corner at
small park.

L on Jackson St., one block.
L at first corner, by small
triangle shaped park.
R on James St. to Light Rail.
Entrance is on left side
of the street.

fallen
fighters
memorial

Directions to start:
By car: From I-5 south, Exit 164B.
R on 4th Av. S. First **R** on Brougham.
R at end. Parking under bridge.
OR **R** on Jackson. **R** on 2nd
in to Quest parking lot.

From I-5 north Exit 165B
on to Union. **L** at 5th Av. N.
R on Madison to end.
Parking under bridge.
OR from Madison, **L** on 2nd
to Quest parking lot.

Bus. Free ride area from downtown
Bus 1, 2, 3, 4, 13, 16
Light rail. Pioneer Square.

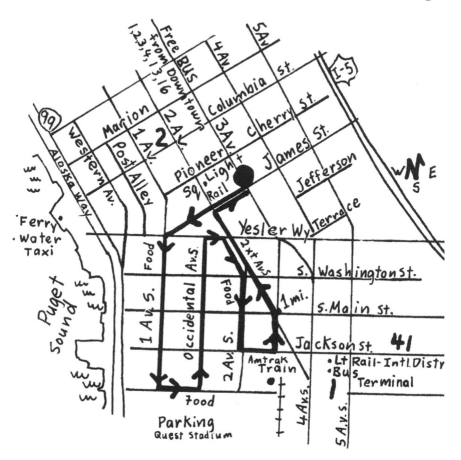

Pioneer Sq. to Pike Place

Distance: 1.5 miles or 2.2 miles
Start: Pioneer Square Light Rail
     Exit to 3rd Ave. and James St.

Light Rail Symbol

Walk downhill on James Street.
R on 1st Ave.
L on Marion, over bridge.
Down steps. L at street.

R on University St, opposite Argosy.
Up steps, half way to top.
L in to Post Alley.
Curves up to Pike Place.
L to market.
R along open-air stalls.
Continue on street one block
You are on Pike Place St.
Cross to opposite side of street.
Return for 1 1/2 block.

Wall of chewing Gum
Add your own!

At white posts with red bands
at street, make a sharp
L in to Post Alley
R at end, up 1/2 steep block.
R on 1st. L on Pine.

Green Tortoise Hostel

Cross 4th Av. to Westlake Center.
(for 1.5 mi. option, take Light
  Rail to Pioneer Sq.)
R on 4th Av.
R on James, 1 block to
  Light Rail.

Library – go to 10th floor for view.

17

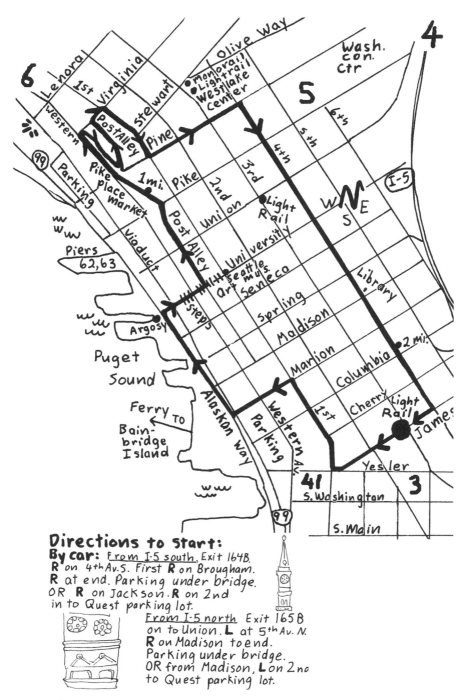

6 Lenora / 1st / Virginia / western / Post Alley / Pike Place market / Parking / (99) / Piers 62,63 / Argosy / Puget Sound / Ferry To / Bainbridge Island / Viaduct

Stewart / Pine / Pike / 1mi. / Post Alley / 2nd / Union / University / steps / 1st / Western Av. / Alaskan Way Parking

Olive Way / monorail / Lightrail / Westlake Center / 3rd / 4th / 5th / 6th / (I-5) / Light Rail / Seattle Art Mus. / Seneca / Spring / Madison / Marion / Columbia / Library / 2 mi. / Cherry / Light Rail / James / Yesler

Wash. con. Ctr

5

W N E S

4

41 / S. Washington / S. Main / **3**

(99)

Directions to start:
By car: From I-5 south, Exit 164B.
R on 4th Av. S. First **R** on Brougham.
R at end. Parking under bridge.
OR **R** on Jackson. **R** on 2nd
in to Quest parking lot.

From I-5 north Exit 165B
on to Union. **L** at 5th Av. N.
R on Madison to end.
Parking under bridge.
OR from Madison, **L** on 2no
to Quest parking lot.

Bus. Free ride area from downtown
Bus 1,2,3,4,13,16
Light rail. Pioneer Square.

Pike Market to Historic Homes

Distance: 2.5 miles, 256 ft. elevation

Start/finish: Pike Place Market

Restrooms in Market.

Walk uphill on Pike St.
R on Bellevue Av.
Straight onto Minor Av.
R on Spring Av, one block.
L on Boren Av.

1117 Minor

Dearborn House

R on Columbia St. 2 blocks.
R on 9 Av. 2 blocks.
L on Madison Av.
R on 5 Av.
L on Pike St.

original cobble stone

mT. Rainer

Directions to start. Pike Place Market
car: <u>from I-5 north:</u> Exit 168B to Union St.
R on 1 Av. **L** on Lenora St.
L on Western Av to parking garage, on **R**.
from I-5 south: Exit 164A toward Dearborn St.
Follow signs to I-5, to Madison St.
L on Madison St. **R** on Western Av.
Light rail: Westlake. Walk on block on 4 Av.
R on Pike to Market.

5

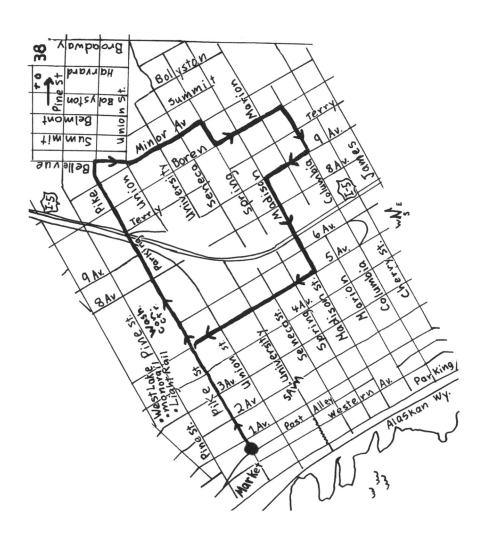

Pike Mkt. to Olympic Sculptures

Distance: 2.3 miles. 90 ft. elevation
Start/finish: Pike Market at 1st Av.
Exit Market on Pike St.
L on 1st Av. **L** on Broad, 1 block
R at Western into Olympic
Sculpture Garden.
R down ramp. **L** up steps at end.
　　　　R on main path, curves around.
　　　　L at end, down to water front.
　　　　L along water.
　　　　To visit P-Patch garden,
　　　　L on Vine 1 block, return.
　　　　Continue along water.

Art in Park

Just before Seattle Aquarium,
L on Pine St. Up steps or
elevator on **L** to Market.

Directions to start. Pike Place Market
car: <u>from I-5 north</u>: Exit 168B to Union St.
　　　R on 1 Av. **L** on Lenora St.
　　　L on Western Av. to parking garage, on **R**.
from I-5 south: Exit 164A toward Dearborn St.
Follow signs to I-5, to Madison st.
L on Madison St. **R** on Western Av.
Light rail: Westlake. Walk on block on 4 Av.
　　　　R on Pike to Market.

21

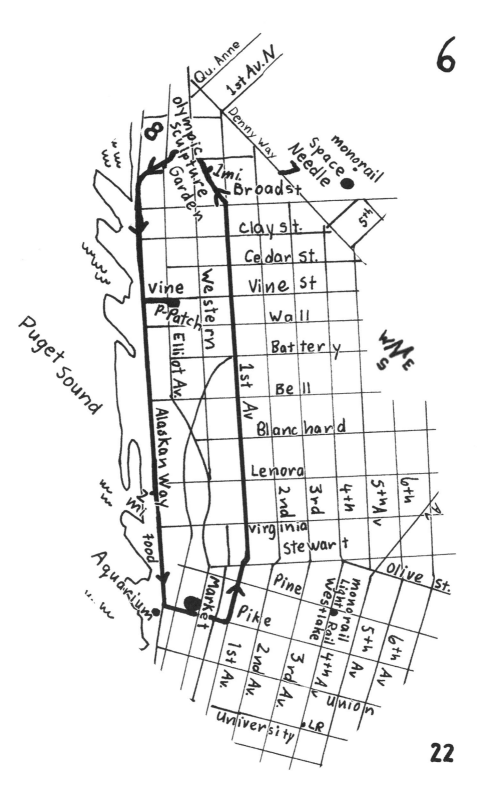

Space Needle to Pike Market

Distance: 1.3 mile - return on monorail
2.7 mile. 180 ft. gradual up. steep down

start / finish: Space Needle, Seattle Center
At Broad st. and 4th, with your
back to the Space Needle,
go R on Broad st.
L on Western Av.
Cross Vine, go R. Explore P-Patch.

L on Elliot Av. R on Wall st.
Cross Alaskan Way, go L.
Just before the Sea. Aqarium
L on Pike St. Take steps or
elevator on left up to market.
on 5th Explore market.

Exit the market on Pike st.
Straight, cross 4th, go L.
(At westlake center, take
monorail for 1.3 mi. walk.)
R on Pine St, 2 blocks.
L on 6th, 1 block.
L on Olive, 1 block.
Cross Westlake Av.
Veer R on 5th, beside
overhead monorail track.

garden
sculpture

L on Wall, 1 block.
R on 4th Av. to Space Needle.

MARKET
GRILL

23

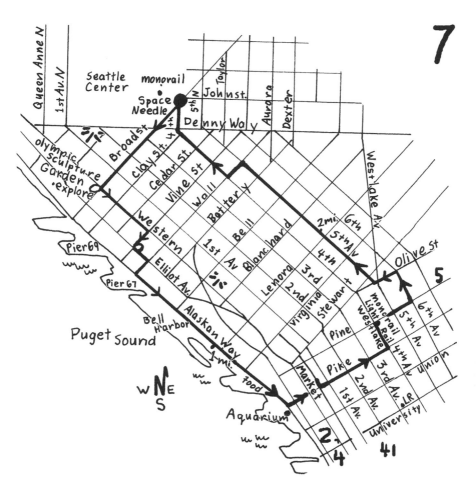

Directions to start. *Space Needle*
Seattle Center, Parking lot at 5 Av. N and Broad St.
car: <u>from Downtown</u>. Find your way to the
waterfront. Go **R** on Alaskan Way.
Turns into Broad St. **L** on 5 Av. N go
2 blocks. **R** into parking lot. Walk across
4 Av. N. in to Center on Harrison.
<u>from I-5 north and south</u>: Exit 167 to
Seattle Center. Follow signs to Seattle Center.
R on 5 Av. N. Go 2 blocks. **R** into parking lot.
bus: from Downtown, 3. Exit at 5 Av. and Broad.
monorail: from Westlake Center. 400 Pine St.
light rail: take Light Rail to Westlake. Transfer
to monorail.
From Parking Lot on 5 Av. N. Walk across 4 Av. N.
Enter Seattle Center on Harrison, to monorail. **24**

Space Needle to Elliot Bay

Distance: 3.5 miles. 200 ft. elevation

Start/finish: Space Needle, at 4th and Broad St.
         Restrooms in Elliot Bay Park.
On Broad, your back to the
Space Needle, go L, 1 block.
L on 5th N. L on Republican.
Curves to 4th N. L on Roy.
         At end, down path in Kinnear Park
         R on Elliot Av. W.
         L on Prospect. Over bridge.
         L along water. (R to rest rooms)
Veer L up ramp into
Olympic Sculpture Gardens.
Take main path over streets.
L down steps to sunken garden.
Up past building. L up Broad St.

Directions to start. Space Needle
Seattle Center, Parking lot at 5 Av. N and Broad St.
car: <u>from Downtown</u>: Find your way to the
         waterfront. Go R on Alaskan Way.
         Turns into Broad St. L on 5 Av. N go
         2 blocks. R into parking lot. Walk across
         4 Av. N. in to Center on Harrison.
<u>from I-5 north and south</u>: Exit 167 to
Seattle Center. Follow signs to Seattle Center.
R on 5 Av. N. Go 2 blocks. R into parking lot.
bus: from Downtown, 3. Exit at 5 Av. and Broad.
monorail: from Westlake Center. 400 Pine St.
light rail: take Light Rail to Westlake. Transfer
         to monorail.
From Parking Lot on 5 Av. N, Walk across 4 Av. N.
Enter Seattle Center on Harrison, to monorail.

25

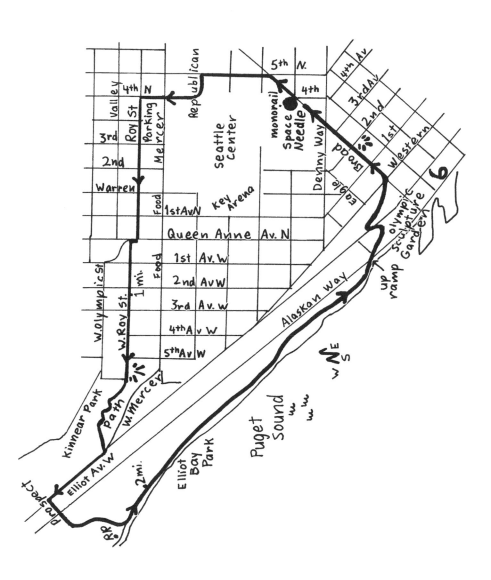

8

Queen Anne West

Distance: 6 miles. 256 ft. gradual up, steep down.
Start/finish: At the monorail by *Space Needle.*

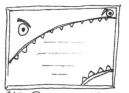

615 Raye Window
Scott Ward Art

Walk up hill past Fun Forest.
Straight at exit on to Thomas st.
R on 1st Av. N. L on Roy, 1 block.
Cross Queen Anne Av. veer
R on sidewalk at Q.Anne WAY,
along Queen Anne Av.
Curves up to Olympic Pl.

At curve to R, cross street
to enter Kinnear Park.
Take upper path. After
restrooms, at fork go R,
up to street. L at street (8th)
Curves on to 10th.

L on Galer. Cross 11th, go R.
R on Howe, 1 block. L on 10th.
R on Wheeler. L on 8th.
R on Raye. R on 5th.
R on McGraw. Cross 7th, go L.

115 olympic

R down Blaine, not the steep street!
Curves L onto Highland Dr.
At Highland, tour Parsons Garden
on your L. Continue on Highland.
on Right side. Cross Q.Anne Av.

Curve R on Prospect.
Curve L on Bigelow. walk on
grass on Right side.
R down Comstock. L at fork in
park. Down any paved path.
R at street (5th).
R into Seattle Center after
Experience Music.

27

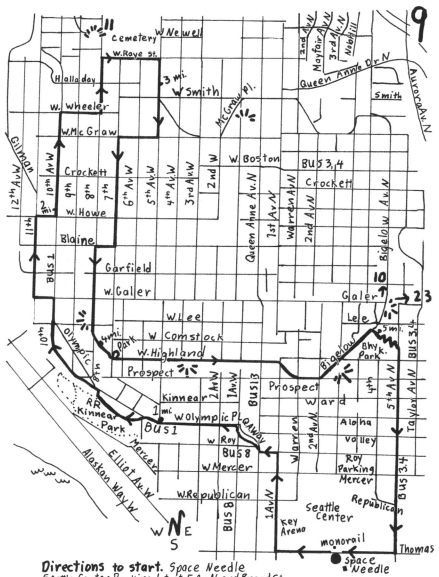

9

Directions to start. *Space Needle*
Seattle Center, Parking lot at 5 Av. N and Broad St.
car: *From Downtown*. Find your way to the
waterfront. Go **R** on Alaskan Way.
Turns into Broad St. **L** on 5Av.N go
2 blocks. **R** into parking lot. Walk across
4Av.N. in to Center on Harrison.
from I-5 north and south: Exit 167 to
Seattle Center. Follow signs to Seattle Center.
R on 5 Av. N. Go 2 blocks. **R** into parking lot.
bus: from Downtown, 3. Exit at 5Av. and Broad.
monorail: from Westlake Center. 400 Pine St.
light rail: take Light Rail to Westlake. Transfer
to monorail.
From Parking Lot on 5Av.N. Walk across 4 Av. N.
Enter Seattle Center on Harrison, to monorail.

Queen Anne Crown

Distance: 1.8 miles. 124 ft. elevation

start/finish: East Queen Anne Playground at Howe St. and Warren Av. N.
Free parking. Seasonal restrooms.

Walk uphill on Warren St.
L on Galer. Down stairs.
L at first street, Bigelow Av. N.

mt Adams
mt. Baker

R on Lynn St, one block.
Enjoy the view.
Return to Bigelow, go **R**.
L on McGraw St.
Cross bridge.
L on Warren Av. N.

Directions to Start.

Car From I-5 north
Exit 172 on to N. 85 St.
L on Aurora Av. N. After bridge,
R on Queen Anne Dr. **L** on 1 Av. N.
L on Howe St. to park.

From I-5 south.
Exit 164B. **R** on 4 Av. S.
First **R** on Royal Brougham.
Second **R** on 1 Av. S. **R** on WA-99 N.
R on Halladay. **L** on 6 Av. N.
Curves into Queen Anne DRIVE.
L on 1 Av. N.
L on Howe St. to park.

Bus From downtown, Bus 4.

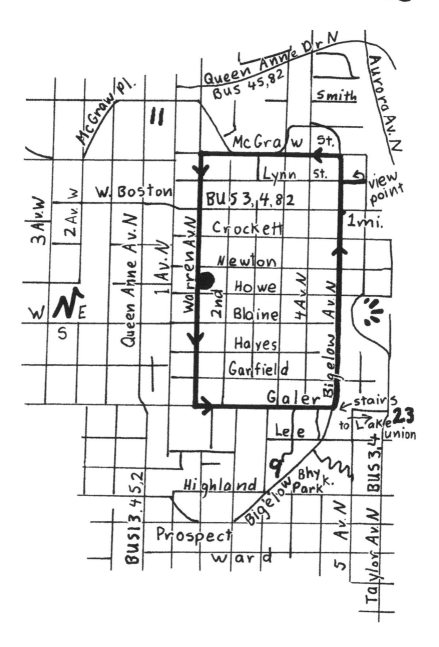

10

McGraw pl.

Queen Anne Dr N
Bus 45,82

Smith

Aurora Av. N

11

McGraw St.

Lynn St.

view point

W. Boston

BUS 3,4,82

Crockett

1mi.

3 Av. W

2 Av. W

Queen Anne Av. N

1 Av. N

Warren Av N

Newton

2nd

Howe

4 Av. N

Bigelow Av. N

Blaine

W

N
E

S

Hayes

Garfield

Galer

stairs
to Lake
union

23

Lee

Highland

Bigelow Bhy
Park.

BUS 3,4

5 Av. N

Taylor Av. N

BUS 13,45,2

Prospect

Bigelow

ward

5

Queen Anne North

Distance: 2.5 miles. 300 ft. elevation

Star t/finish: on 3 Av. N at Nickerson St.
Opposite Bleitz Funeral Home.
Street parking on 3 Av. N, uphill
side of Nickerson St.
No public restrooms.

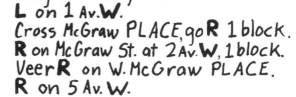

No. Cascades

Walk uphill on 3 Av. N. **R** on Newell.
L on Mayfair, one block.
R up stairs to Mayfair Park.
Through park. Straight on Raye St.
L on 1 Av. **W.**
Cross McGraw PLACE, go **R** 1 block.
R on McGraw St. at 2 Av. W, 1 block.
Veer **R** on W. McGraw PLACE.
R on 5 Av. **W.**

SPU

R down stairs at Dravis.
Straight into Seattle Pacific campus.
R down steps between first two
buildings. After first building,
(Moyer Hall) veer **R** to flagpole.
Around the circle (Tiffany Loop).
Through the arch.
L on 3 Av. N, to the canal.

cute house
award

4 Raye

R at W. Ewing mini-park.
on to gravel path along canal.
R up ramp before
Fremont bridge.
Cross Nickerson St.
Straight on to 3 Av. N.

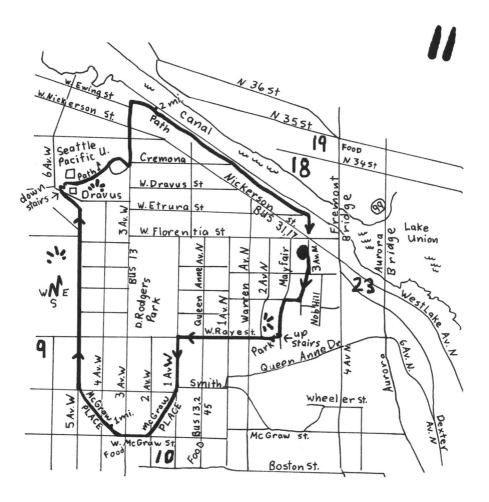

Directions to start. near Fremont Bridge, on 3 Av. N. at Nickerson, opposite Bleitz Funeral.'
car: from I-5 north or south: Exit 167 toward Seattle Center. **L** to stay on Fairway. **L** on Valley st. **R** on Westlake Av. N. At Bleitz Funeral Home, **L** on 3 Av N.
bus: from Downtown, 26 to Dexter Av. and 4 Av. N. Walk to 3 Av. N., go **L** up 3 Av.

Magnolia to Discovery Park

Distance: 1 mi. flat. 2.6 mi, 5 mi, 243 ft. elevation
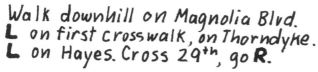 6.8 mi. 243 ft. elevation gain TWICE.

Start/finish: Magnolia Park, Between Magnolia
Bridge and Howe, on Magnolia Blvd.
Free parking. Seasonal restrooms.

Walk downhill on Magnolia Blvd.
L on first crosswalk, on Thorndyke.
L on Hayes. Cross 29th, go **R**.

For 2.6 mi. and 5 mi:
L down Condon. **L** on McGraw.
Jog **L** on 34th, **R** on Viewmont.
for 5 mi. route, see ★ below.

for 2.6 mi. route, BEFORE the
big **R** curve, **L** down Constance.
R on 36th N, one block.
R on 36th W. Cross street go **L**.
See ■ below.

L on Emerson, one block.
(South Entrane to Discovery
Park is one more block.)
L on Magnolia Blvd., curves.
■ Cross bridge on Howe St.
R on Magnolia Blvd.

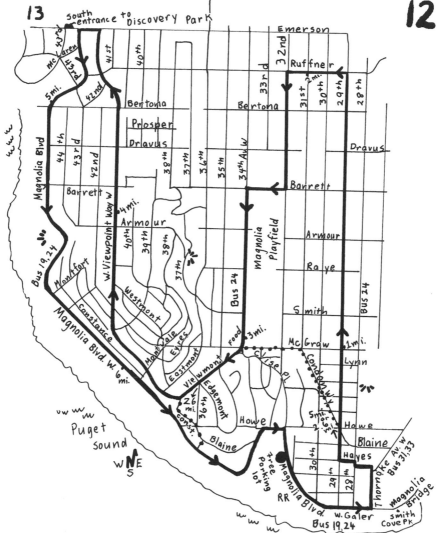

Directions to start. Magnolia Park
1461 Magnolia Blvd. W.

car: <u>from I-5 north and south:</u> Exit 167 to
Seattle Center, to Fairview. **L** on Valley St.
onto Broad St. **R** on Denny Way, to
Western Av. W, to Elliot Av. Turn **R**.
R to cross Magnolia Bridge.
Straight to Magnolia Blvd. W. **L** into Park.

bus: from Downtown, 24. Exit on 28 Av. W
at Hayes St. to join enroute.

Discovery Park

Start/finish: South parking lot off W. Emerson
at 43 Av. W. Free parking.
Portable toilets.

Historic Parade Grounds

Distance: 1.5 miles, 98 ft. elevation

Walk back to entrance, go
R past bollards. Take lower road.
L at first intersection.
R at end. Cross next road, go
about 50 paces, **R** up steps.
Take upper road, to yellow hydrant.

old stables

R on path at fire hydrant.
Go to flagpole.
View parade grounds.

gymnasium

Continue on path, to church.
R on path around church.
Just before the end of the stone
wall, **L** on path.

2.8 mile Trail Loop

242 ft. elevation ━ ━ ━ trail route on map.

Find the trail markers near
the start of the parking lot.
Follow markers. There are
other roads and trails, but
it is well-marked.

church

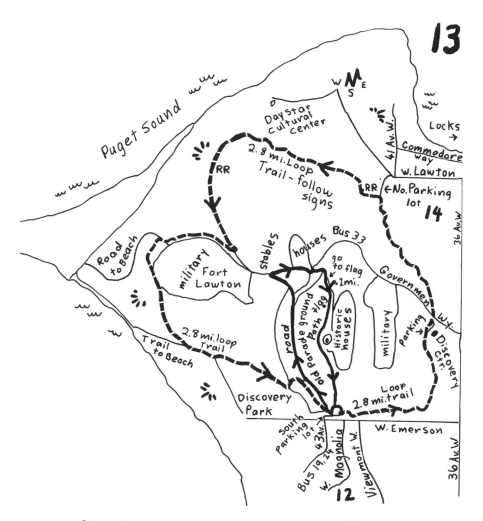

13

Directions to start. Discovery Park, go to
South Parking Lot at 43 Av.W and W.Emerson St.
car: <u>from I-5 north</u>: Exit 173 to Northgate Way.
R on Northgate, becomes N.105 st.
Veer **L** on Holman Rd. Veer **L** on 15 Av. NW.
Veer **R** on W.Emerson. **R** on Gilman,
becomes W.Government Way. **L** on 34 Av.W.
R on W.Emerson. **R** into park at 43 Av.
<u>from I-5 south</u>: Exit 164A to Madison St.
L on Madison St. **R** on Alaskan Way.
Follow to Elliot Av. Get in **R** Lane to cross
Magnolia Bridge. **L** at Howe St.
L on Magnolia Blvd.W. **L** on Emerson. **R** to Park.
bus: from Downtown, 24.

Locks to Discovery Park

Distance: 1.5 mi., 3 mi. or 3.7 mi. 236 ft. elevation

Start/finish: Commodore Park on W. Commodore. on Crittendon Locks. Free parking. Restrooms at locks.

From park, cross street to sidewalk. Walk under railroad bridge. **R** on 40th. At end, curve **R** onto 39th. **R** on Cramer, ½ block. **L** on 40th. (for 1.5 mi. **L** on Commodore to Park)

Before Discovery Park sign, **L** down W. Lawton St. Down stairs at end. **R** on 36th. At 3501 w. Ohman Place, **L** on short loop in Kiwanis park (for 3 mi. option, **L** down Government Way. See *below)

L on Thurman St. **L** on 33rd. **R** on Elmore. Down steps at end. **L** at street, 30th. **L** on Jameson, ½ block. Cross Government Way, go **R**, on to bike path.*

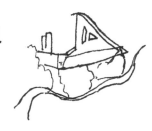

Down path into Commodore Park. **R** in park, down path to locks. **L** at fish ladder, along canal.

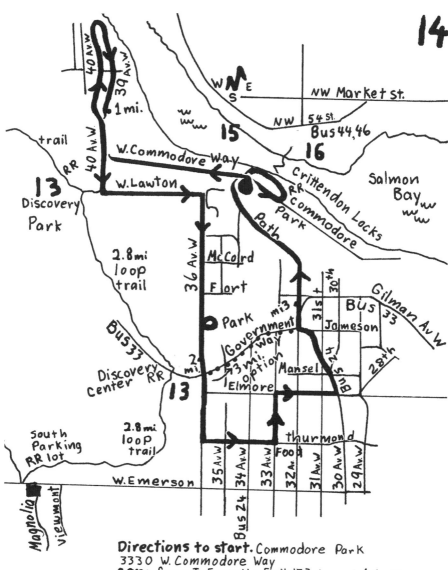

14

NW Market st.

NW 54 St.
Bus 44,46

W N E S

15

16

1 mi.

40 Av.W

39 Av.W

W. Commodore Way

Crittendon Locks

Salmon Bay

trail

RR

40 Av.W

13
Discovery
Park

W. Lawton

RR Commodore

Path

Park

2.8 mi
loop
trail

36 Av.W

McCord

F ort

Park

Government Way

mi3

31st

30th

Gilman Av.W

BUS 33

Jameson

Bus 33

Discovery
Center RR

13

2.
mi.

.3 mi.
option

Elmore

Mansel

Bus 24

28th

2.8 mi
loop
trail

south
Parking
RR lot

35 Av.W

34 Av.W

33 Av.W

Food

thurmond

32 Av.

31 Av.W

30 Av.W

29 Av.W

W. Emerson

Magnolia

viewmont

Bus 24

Directions to start. Commodore Park
3330 W. Commodore Way
car: <u>from I-5 north</u>: Exit 173 toward 1 Av. NE
   R on Northgate Way. Curves onto N. 105 st.
   L on Holman. Curves on to 15 Av. NW.
   After bridge, **R** on Emerson. **R** on 21 Av.
   Curves **L** on Commodore. **R** at Park.
<u>from I-5 south</u>: Exit 167 to Seattle Center.
On to Fairview, get in **L** lane, **L** on Valley st.
R on Westlake Av. N. Curves into Nickerson.
Jog **L** on 13 Av. W, then **R** on Nickerson.
Take Emerson Ramp. **L** on W. Emerson.
R on 21 Av. W. Curves into W. Commodore.
R into Commodore Park.
bus: from Downtown, 17. Exit at 32 Av. on 54 St.
   Walk across Locks into Comm. Park.

Golden Gardens Park

Distance: 1mi. to 4.75 miles. Flat
Start/finish: NW 54th and 32nd Av. NW
              Free parking on NW 54th.
              (for 1 mi. start at the Park)
              Visit the Locks or Botanical Garden.

With your back to the Locks,
 go **L** on path along street.
L on Sea View St, off path.
L in to Shilsole Port.
R along marina on sidewalk.
L around big chain link fence.
              Continue into park, on path.
              After brick building, **L** path.
              At end, **L** to return along beach.
              At park exit, cross street to
              return on bike path.

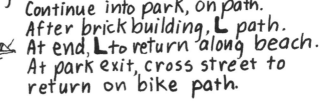

Directions to start: Ballard Locks

car: <u>from Downtown Seattle.</u> West on Denny Way.
       Curves **R** into Elliot Av, into 15 Av. NW.
       L on Market st. **L** on 54 st. Pay parking.
       Free street parking on 57 St, off 32 Av.
from I-5 north: Exit 172, to 85 St.
              First **R**, on 24 Av, **L** on 54 St.
from I-5 south: Exit 169. **L** on NE 45 St.
              Follow signs to Locks.
bus: from Downtown, 17 to NW 54 st at 32 Av. NW.

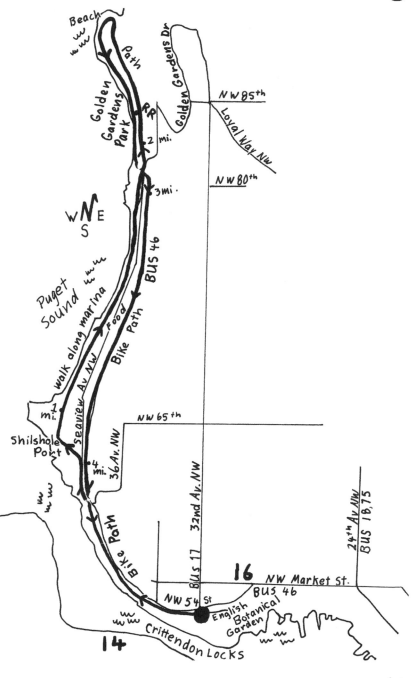

Beach

Path

Golden Gardens Park

Golden Gardens Dr

RR

2 mi.

NW 85th

Loyal Way NW

NW 80th

3 mi.

W N E
S

Puget Sound

walk along marina

Seaview Av NW

Food

Bike Path

BUS 46

1 mi.

Shilshole Point

36 Av. NW

4 mi.

NW 65th

32nd Av. NW

24th Av. NW

BUS 18, 75

Bike Path

Bus 17

16 NW Market St.

BUS 46

NW 54 St

English Botanical Garden

14

Crittendon Locks

The Best of Ballard

Distance: ½ mile around Gardens and Locks.
2 mile, to 17th and return.
3 mile flat or 6.4 mi. 348 ft. elevation

Start/finish: Crittendon Locks on 54 St. at 32nd Av NW
history plaques   Pay parking. OR free parking across
the locks at Commodore Park.
Rest rooms across the locks.

Facing the locks, go **L** on 54 St,
Curves into Market St.
R on Ballard Av. At 17 Av, cross
Ballard and return on other side.

Curves **R** on 22 Av, one block.
R on Market st. At 20 Av, **L** to
cross and return to 22nd.
R on 22nd. **L** on 57 st, veering
R through park on diagonal.
R on 24 Av. **L** on 60 st. one block.

562

for 3 mi. continue on 60 St.
L on 28 Av. **R** on Market to 54 St.

door handles

L on 80 St. **R** on Loyal Way.
(at 32nd-optional steps down
to Golden Gardens Park.)
L on 32nd.   **R** on 80 St.
L on 33rd.   **R** on 77th.
L on 34th.

view of Mt. Rainer

L on Market st., one block.
R on 32nd.

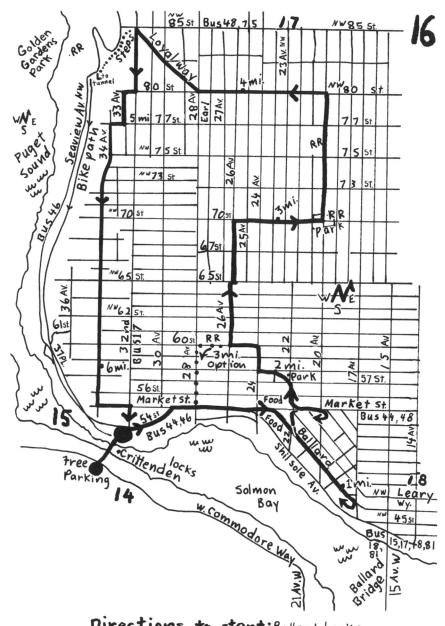

16

Directions to start: Ballard Locks

car: *from Downtown Seattle* West on Denny Way.
Curves R into Elliot Av, into 15 Av. NW.
L on Market St. L on 54 St. Pay parking.
Free street parking on 57 St, off 32 Av.
from I-5 north: Exit 172, to 85 St.
First R, on 24 Av, L on 54 St.
from I-5 south. Exit 169. L on NE 45 St.
Follow signs to Locks.
bus: from Downtown, 17 to NW 54 St at 32 Av. NW.

Christmas Lights

Distance: 1.1 miles or 2.1 miles.
128 ft. elevation, gradual and easy.

Decorated in December. Lovely walk all year.
Free street parking. No restrooms.

Enter from NW 85th, on to 23rd Av. NW
into Olympic Manor subdivision.
Take first **R**, on to 86th. Park here.

Walk up 86th. **L** on 21st.
L on 94th. Curves into 22nd.
Curve **R** into 87th.
(for 1.1 mi, **L** on 23rd.)
(**L** on 86th to your car.)
R on 23rd.

L down 94th and return to 23rd.
Go back on 23rd.
Cross 89th, go **R** one block.
L on Jones. Curves into 23rd.

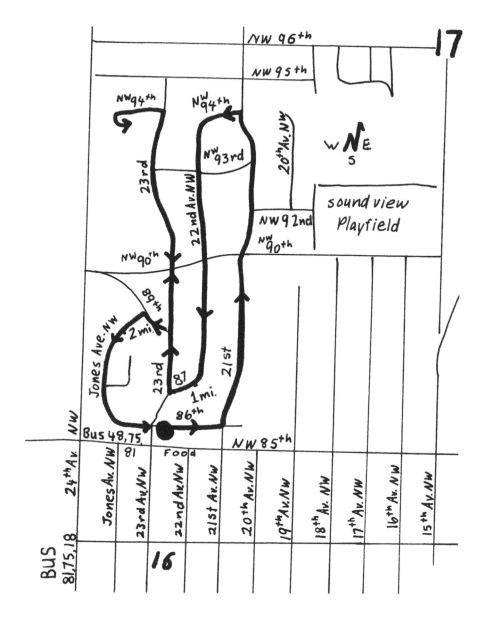

17

Directions to start. N. 85 st. and 23 Av. NW

car: <u>from I-5 north:</u> Exit 172 to N 85 st.
<u>from I-5 south:</u> Exit 172 to N 85 st, go
toward Aurora A. Veer **L** on N 85 st.

bus: from Downtown, 18 toward North Beach.

Fremont and Ballard Bridges

Note: The Ballard side is industrial and I think it
is interesting. If you prefer quiet beauty,
walk out and back along each side of the
canal on the Fremont bridge end.

Distance: 4.2 miles. 50 ft. elevation over bridge.
Start/finish: Evanston Av. N. and N. 34th St.
No public restrooms. Free street
parking en route on Canal St.

Walk downhill on Evanston,
R along canal on path.

L on 45th along railroad tracks.
R on 11th Av. NW.
L on NW Leary Way.
Under bridge. Cross 15th.
Up and over Ballard Bridge.

R down first steps. Do not turn
right and cross next bridge.
R on path. **R** under bridge.
Cross street to walk on left side.
You emerge on Nickerson.

L on 11th, 1 block.
R on street (W. Ewing).
Through park, straight on
to canal path.

FIRE
Dragon
Marine
training

King Co. Environ. Lab

Gaia's
Gift

R up ramp to Fremont, before the
bridge, to street.
L at corner to Blietz Funeral Home.
L across Fremont Bridge.
L on 34th to Evanston.

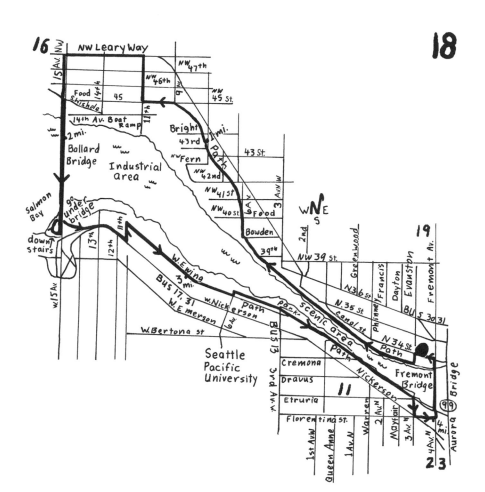

Directions to start. Fremont AvN at 34 St.N

car: from I-5 north: Exit 169 to NE 45 st.
        R on NE 45 st. **L** on Stoneway.
        R on 34 st. to Fremont. Parking garage
        is under Aurora bridge.
from I-5 south: Exit 167 to Mercer St.
R on Fairview Av. N. **L** on Valley.
R on Westlake. Veer **R** on 4, over bridge.
R on 34 St. Parking garage under Aurora bridge
bus: from downtown, 5 toward Northgate.
        Exit at 39 St. Walk down Fremont to 34 st.

Fremont to Woodland Park

Distances: 2, 3, 4.5 or 5.5 miles. 370 ft. elevation
   See map for shorter mileages.
Start/finish: N. 34th and Evanston Av. N.
   (parking garage on 34th under big bridge)

Walk downhill on Evanston to canal.
R on canal path. R on street
AFTER 36th, opposite silos to light.
Up 39th? L on Linden.
   L on 46th 1 block. R on Fremont.
   Cross 50th. R into Rose Garden.
   Circle L to exit.
   R on path along road.
   L after brown building on to
   path to Lower Woodland, Green Lk.

46th + Phinney

Olympic Mt.

After bridge over street,
L on farthest L path. Stay on
main path to restroom building.
Sharp L up small path.
Cross pedestrian bridge.
R on path.   L on 60th.

Bonsai trees

   L on Evanston. Curve R thru park.
   L on Greenwood. L on 46th, 1 block
   Cross Phinney, go R 1 block.
   L on 45th. R on Evanston.
   L at end. Down steps. R ½ block.
   L across Fremont, go R.
L on 36th to Troll. R down Troll Av.
R on 34th. R on Fremont, 1 block.
Cross 35th, go L then
Veer R on Fremont PLACE.
L on Evanston to 34th.

mural in tunnel

Troll

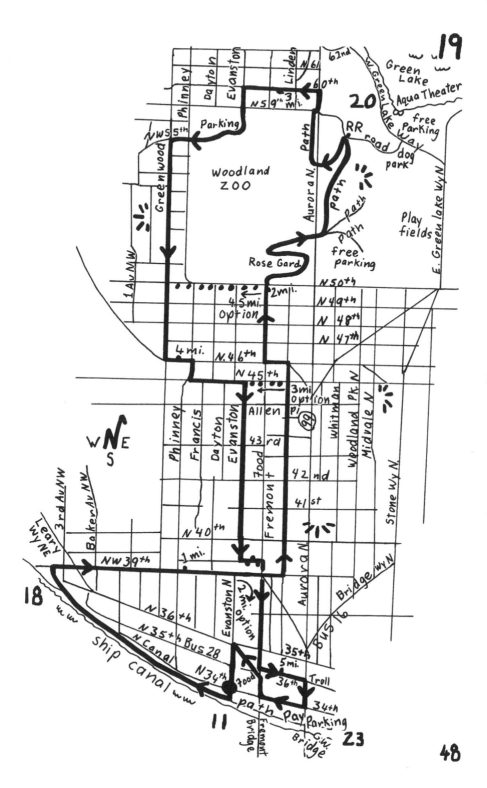

Green Lake to Greenwood

Distance: 2 mi. easy, 3.7 mi. or 5 mi. 122 ft. elevation

Start/finish: Aqua Theater on W. Greenlake Way
at Woodland Park.
Free parking, restrooms.

Face the theater, go **L** on path ½ mi.
Look **L** for crosswalk sign.
Use it to cross the street, Aurora.
Jog **L** then **R** on 68th.
R on Fremont.
 (for 2 mi., return at 72nd.)
L on 83rd. (for 3.7 mi. **R** on 83rd.
 see * below.)

Cross Greenwood Av., go **R**.
R on 87th across Greenwood.
R to return along Greenwood.
L on 84th.

R on Linden, one block.
Cross 83rd, go **L**.
At the intersection cross Aurora.
L across Greenlake Dr. N
R on 83rd.
* **R** on Stone ½ block.
L on 82nd.

R on Densmore.
L on 88th one block.
Cross Wallingford, go **R**
to waterfront.
 (for 3.7 mi., **R** on path.)
L on path to Aqua Theater.

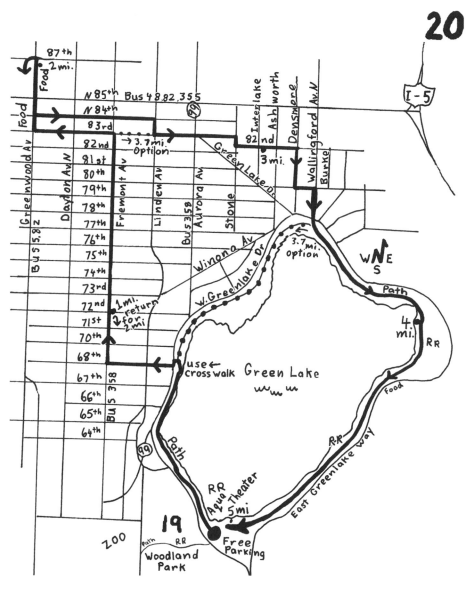

20

Directions to start. Green Lake Aqua Theater

car: <u>from I-5 north</u>: Exit 171 to NE 71st. **R** on 71st. **L** on E.Green Lake Dr. N.
R on W. Gr. Lk. Wy. Parking after golf course.
<u>from I-5 south</u>: Exit 169 to NE 50st. **L** on 50st. **R** on Gr. Lake Wy N. Parking lot after **L** curve.
bus: from Downtown, 358. Exit on Linden at N 68st. See map to join enroute.

Green Lake to Wallingford Park

Distance: 3 miles around Lake. Flat.
5 miles entire route. 113 ft. up

Start/finish: GreenLake Community Center at
E. GreenLake N. and Latona Av.NE
Free parking, restrooms.

R on path along lake.
After the aqua theater, on **R**,
follow path along chain
link fence along golf course.
Curves **R**.
L at street, 1 block.
R on Kenwood on crosswalk.
R up Ashworth Av.

Jog **L** on N 55th, then
R on Woodlawn Av. N
L on 50th, 2 blocks
R on Wallingford Av.

R on N 43rd, 2 blocks.
R on Woodlawn Av. 2 blocks
R on N 45th, 2 blocks
L on Wallingford Av.

L down Kenwood Place.
Cross E. Green Lake Way N.
R along lake to Community center.

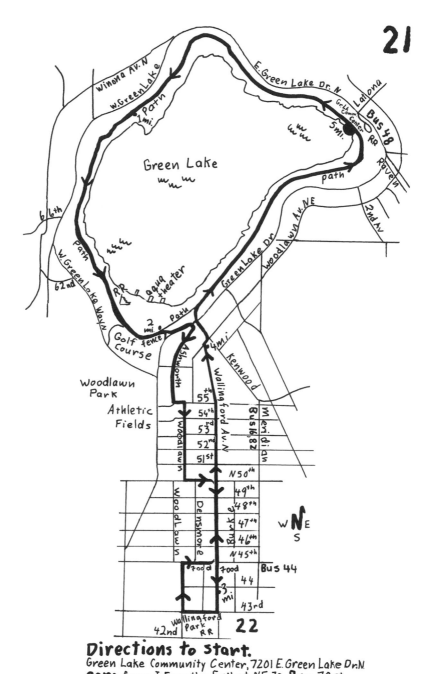

21

Green Lake

Winona Av. N

W. Green Lake Path 1 mi.

E. Green Lake Dr. N

Latona

Gr. Lk. Comm. Center

Bus 48

5 mi.

RR

Raven

2nd Av

path

66th

W. Green Lake Way

62nd

aqua theater

Green Lake Dr

Woodlawn Av. NE

2 mi. Path

Golf Course

fence

.4 mi.

Ashworth

kenwood

Wallingford Av. N

Meridian

Bus 16, 82

Woodlawn Park

Athletic Fields

Woodlawn

55th

54th

53rd

52nd

51st

N 50th

49th

48th

47th

46th

N 45th

Woodlawn

Densmore

Bus K

food

food

Bus 44

44

.3 mi.

43rd

Wallingford Park RR

42nd

22

W **N** E
        S

Directions to start.
Green Lake Community Center, 7201 E. Green Lake Dr. N.

car: <u>from I-5 north:</u> Exit at NE 70. **R** on 70 st.
  R on Gr. Lake Dr. N. to Community Ctr.
  <u>from I-5 south:</u> Exit at 65 st./Ravenna Blvd.
  L on 65 st. **R** on Ravenna for .3 miles.
  R on E. Green Lake Dr. N to Comm. Ctr.

bus: from Downtown, 26 to Latona and
  E. Green Lake Way. from University, 48.

Wallingford Park to Gas Works

Distance: 3 miles. 260 ft. gradual up and down.

Start/finish: N 43 St. and Wallingford Av. N

Free parking on 43 St. Restrooms in Park.
On 43rd, walk along park.
R on Woodlawn Av. N.
R on 45th, 2 blocks
R on Wallingford, 1 block.
L on 43rd, 1 block.
R on Burke Av. N.

L on N 36th, over crosswalk at lake.
R along Lake Union.
At Meridian Av. go straight on path into Gas Works park.
L at first street into park.
R on path around park.

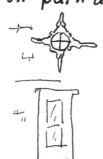

Go to viewpoint past tall, round brown towers.
Take steps down to left.
R along Lake, curve around
L side of hill.
L on main path.
Cross Street.

Jog **R** on Northlake Place, then
L on Densmore, 2 blocks.
L on 35th, one block.
R on Woodlawn to 43rd.

Animal sculpture

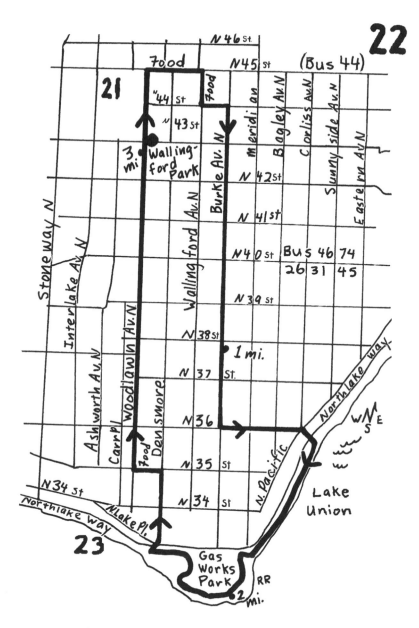

Directions to start. Wallingford Park on Wallingford Av. N between N 42 st. and N 43 st.

car: from I-5: Exit 169 to N 45 St.
   from North, **R** on 45 St. from South, **L** on 45 St.
   L on Wallingford. **R** on 43 St. Park here.

bus: from Downtown, 45, 26. Exit at 40 st and Wallingford. Walk 2 blocks up Wallingford.

Lake Union Loop

Distance: 6.3 miles. 113 ft. elevation
Start/finish: Gas Works Park. 2101 N. Northlake
free parking, restrooms

Face park, go L on gravel path,
through trees. where path
ends, cross street to continue
on lower path, not Burke-Gilman.

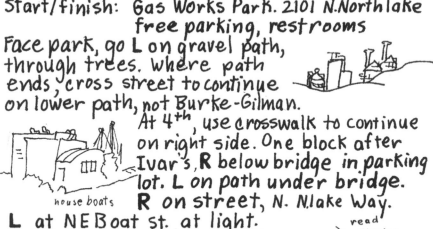

At 4th, use crosswalk to continue
on right side. One block after
Ivar's, R below bridge in parking
lot. L on path under bridge.
house boats   R on street, N. Nlake Way.

L at NE Boat st. at light.
Jog R then L up first path,
between buildings.
L on path to bridge.
R up first steps under bridge.
L on street under bridge.
R up steps to bridge, cross.

read
Stories
on
Railing

R on Fuhrnam. Curves L.
on to Fairview. L on Hamlin, ½blk
R on Yale Terrace. R on Roanoke
Curves L around lake.
Walk
the rail line
Stay close to lake, past Hooters,
thread through shops.

Through Lake Union Park.
along lake, up to cross
Fremont bridge. Immediate
R down steps. L along lake.
on path. At N. Northlake Way,
take this street. At curve veer
R on narrow street to Gas Works.

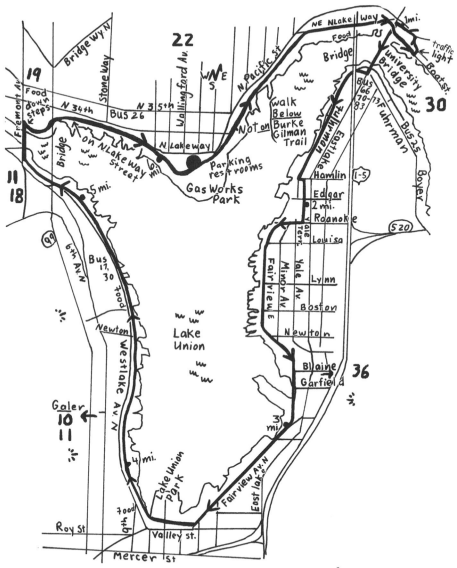

23

Directions to start: Gas Works Park
2101 N. Northlake Way
car: from I-5 north and south. Take 45 St. exit.
Go West on NE 45 St. **L** on Meridian Av. N.
which ends at Gas Works Park.
R on N. Northlake, into the parking lot.
bus: from Downtown, 26. Exit at N 35 st.
at Wallingford. Walk down Wallingford to Park.

Green Lake to U. Washington

Distance: 2.1mi. or 4.1 miles. 342 ft. elevation
start/finish: Green Lake Community Center
                7201 E. Green Lake Dr. N.
                free parking, restrooms

Walk to Green Lake Dr. N.
Up 71st on right side.
Veer **R** over bridge, on to 70 st.
Cross 15 Av., go **R** 2 blocks.
L on 68 st, 2 blocks.
R on 17 Av. Through roundabout.
Veer **L** on Naomi.

R on 20 Av. Over bridge.
(for 2.1 mi. option,
R on Ravenna. See ✶ below.)
R on 55th, 1 short steep block,
 - or **R** on 52 st, less steep.

Calla

L on 19 Av.
R on 45 st, 2 blocks
R on 17 Av.
L on Ravenna Blvd.
✶ Cross Green Lake Dr. N.
 into park.
R in park.
L on tree-lined path.
Rest rooms are on both sides
of building, on outside.

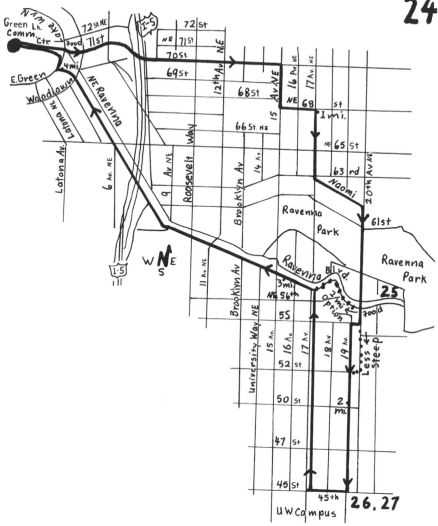

24

Directions to start.
Green Lake Community Center, 7201 E. Green Lake Dr.N.
car: <u>from I-5 north</u>: Exit at NE 70. **R** on 70 st.
R on Gr. Lake Dr. N. to Community Ctr.
<u>from I-5 south</u>: Exit at 65 st./Ravenna Blvd.
L on 65 st. **R** on Ravenna for .3 miles.
R on E. Green Lake Dr. N to Comm. Ctr.
bus: from Downtown, 26 to Latona and
E. Green Lake Way. from University, 48.

Candy Cane Lane

Distance: .2 miles. 33 ft. elevation gain.
Go in December when it is decorated.
Start/finish: Small parking lot off

NE Ravenna Blvd and Ravenna Ave. NE
where street splits to a boulevard.
Free parking. No restroom.

Exit parking lot to street.
R up Ravenna. Boulevard.
R at corner, onto Park Rd. NE.
Go around the circle.
Down Park Rd. **L** at street.

Peace on Earth

Directions to start: use small parking lot
where Ravenna Blvd. and Ravenna Ave. join.
car: from I-5 north: Exit 171 to NE 71st.
veer **L** up 70 st. **R** on Ravenna Blvd. ✳
from I-5 south: Exit 170 for Ravenna, 65 st.
R on Ravenna Blvd. ✳
✳ Just BEFORE curves **R**, steeply down into
Ravenna Av. NE. **L** into small parking lot.
bus: from Downtown, 74, 30. Exit on
Ravenna Boulevard at 21 Av. NE.

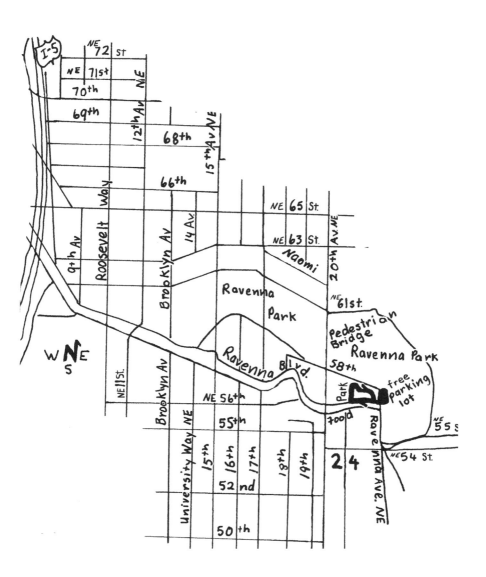

25

UW and the Ave.

Distance: 2 miles. 120 ft. elevation.
Start/finish: Central Plaza, above parking
garage at 15th NE and NE 40th.

At the tall brick towers,
veer **R** down steps, pass
fountain. Take path on right
side down tree-lined path.

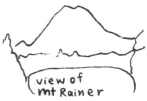

view of
mt Rainer

At the 3 yellow posts in path,
R on gravel path.
At bus stop, veer **R** along
gray shelter. Pass through
medinical gardens, in center.
Exit between 'Monkeys' on post tops

Cross street, go **R**.(stevens Way)
L at Physics/A Building sign.
L down steps, lots of steps.
R on paved bike path, 2 blocks.
R on Brooklyn St. (no sign).
R on Campus Way NE, 1 block.
L on University Way (the Ave.)

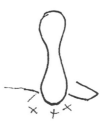

R on 45th. **R** on Memorial Dr.
L on Stevens Way, curves **R**.
R on path to Foster Business Sch.
Pass under walkway bridge.
Veer **L** on path. Stay on diagonal
Down steps.
R on main path in Quad,
to Central Plaza.

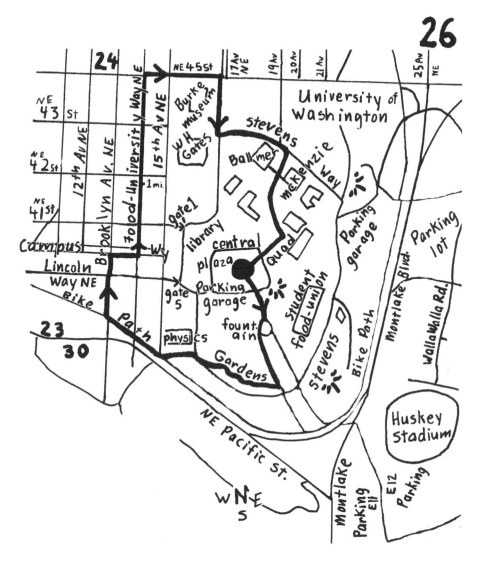

26

Directions to start. U.Washington
Central Plaza over Central parking garage.
car: from I-5 north: Exit 167. **L** on NE 45 St.
    R on 15 Av. NE. **L** on 41 St. into gate 1 lot.
from I-5 south: Exit 169. **R** on 45 St.
R on 15 Av. NE. **L** on 41 St. into gate 1 parking lot.
bus: from Downtown, 73 Express. Exit at
    Campus Parkway and Brooklyn.
    Walk up Campus, across 15 Av. to Plaza.

UW Natural Area

Distance: 4 miles. 160 ft. elevation
Start/finish: Central Plaza. above parking
garage at 15th NE and NE 40th.

At the tall brick towers,
Veer R, down steps. Pass
fountain, down tree-lined path.
L on bike path for 100 ft.
R down stairs. Cross street.

fountain

R at Huskey Stadium gates.
Straight, between E11 and E12
lots, on to grass, to lake.
L on path along lake.
Curves L onto E. Campus Bike path.

R into small E9 lot on gravel path.
(before Walla Walla St.)
R down steps along building.
L along dock of shell house.
Onto gravel path.

fountain
in
Soeste
Garden

R over bridge. Across parking lot.
R on first trail, curves L.
R at first intersection,
(to Botanical Gardens)
R on street to Soeste Garden,
(R off the street.)

Return on street (41st)
Curves into Mary Gates St.
L on NE Clark. Cross parking
lot to far steps. Up and over.
L on bike path.
R up tree-lined path.
Straight to return to Plaza.

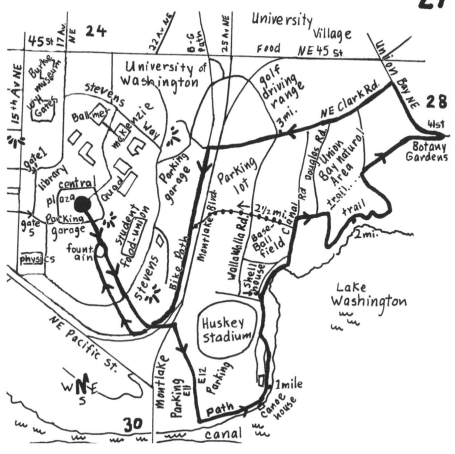

27

Directions to start. U.Washington
Central Plaza over Central parking garage.
car: from I-5 north: Exit 167. **L** on NE 45 St.
R on 15 Av. NE. **L** on 41 St. into gate 1 lot.
from I-5 south: Exit 169, **R** on 45 St.
R on 15 Av. NE. **L** on 41 St. into gate 1 parking lot.
bus: from Downtown, 73 Express. Exit at
Campus Parkway and Brooklyn.
Walk up Campus, across 15 Av. to Plaza.

Laurelhurst

North Cascades view

Distance: 2 mi. 100 ft, or 3.5 mi. 156 ft, or 5.8 mi. 312 ft.

Start/finish: At parking lot next UW Botanical
Gardens at 41 St and 36 Av. NE.
Free parking. Restrooms at L.H. Park

From parking lot, **R** on NE 41 ST.
R on 42 AV. Curves **L** on 43 AV.
(for 2 mi. **L** on 45 ST. **L** on 42 Av.)
Rejoin at ✳ below.

R on 45 ST. **R** up ramp into Park.
Circle **R** around Park.
(for 3.5 mi., exit park at parking
lot. **L** on 41 St. **R** on 48 Av. Rejoin at ✳
Over bridge, across 45 ST.
L on 47 ST, one block. **R** on 46 AV.

cute house award

4311 43rd Av NE

R on 54 ST (**L** on 47, **R** to food).
Curves **R** onto 48 AV.
L on 50 St, one block. **R** on 49 AV.
L on 45 ST. Curves **L** onto 52 AV,
onto W. Laurel Dr. Cross 55 AV. go **R**

Curves onto 41 ST. **L** on 50 AV.
Cross 40 ST. go **R**, one block.
Cross 49 AV, one block, go **L**.
R on 39 ST. **L** on 48 AV. onto 47 Pl

✳ **L** on E. Laurelhurst Dr. Curves.
L on 33 ST, one block.
Curve **R** on 43 AV. **L** on 42 AV.

At 3657-42 AV go **L** down path
to Belvoir Pl. Park to shore, return
✳ **L** on Surber Dr.
L on 41 ST.

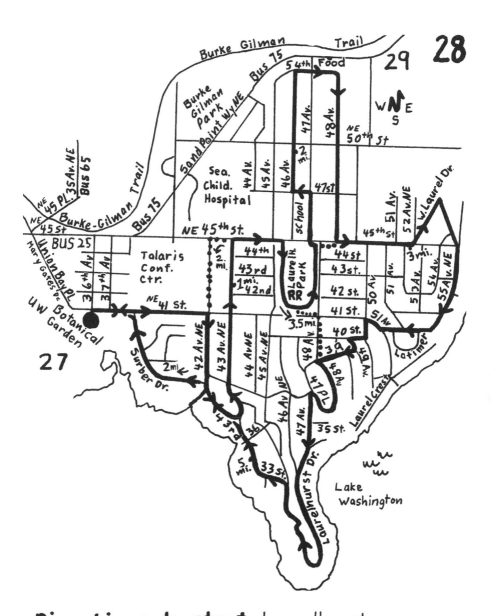

28

Directions to start. Laurelhurst
NE 41 St. at Union Bay PL, NE, parking lot.
car: from I-5 north or south: Exit 169 to 45 st.
East on 45 st (**L** from the north, **R** from south)
R on Mary Gates Dr. Curves into 41 St.
R in to parking lot after curve.
bus: from Downtown, 25, Exit at 43 Av. the
Children's Hospital to join enroute.

Burke-Gilham Park to Magnuson Park

Distance: 1 mi. easy on Burke-Gilman Trail to 65 St.
          2 mi. easy. Start/finish in Magnuson Park,
           parking lot on 65 St. See * below.
          6.1 mi.   184 ft. gain.

Start/finish: Burke-Gilman Park at NE 52 St. and
              Sand Point Way NE. Free parking.
              Seasonal restrooms.

Walk downhill on path.
R at fork. **R** onto Burke-Gilman Tr.
After bridge, **R** up path.
Cross street, go **L** on Sand
Point Way. (**R** to food.)

R on Windemere. **L** up 55 st.
L on 60 Av. **R** on 57 ST.
L on 63 Av. **R** on 60 ST.
L on 65 Av. Opposite sign to
Brad. Ct. Office, **R** through gate
in fence to Promotory Pt. area.
R to upper trail. **R** at fork in old road.
Stay along fence. At 3 forks, take
middle one down.
R on road*L along shoreline.
Cross boat ramp. Take paved
path. **L** at end, along dog park.

to view point
at lakeside

Curves **L** to upper road.
Up first path on **R**.
L along athletic fields.
L at first opportunity, to restroom.
R on main path. **L** at next fork.
Weave through wetlands.
R on path along street (65 st.)
Exit park. **L** on Burke-Gilman Trail.

67

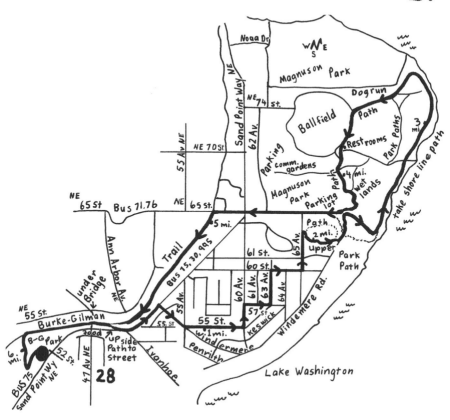

29

Directions to start:

Burke-Gilman Park, 5201 SandPoint Way NE

car: <u>from I-5 north</u>: Exit 169 to 45 st.
　　　L on NE 45 St. Curves onto Sand Point Way.
　　　L at 52 St. into Burke-Gilman Park.
<u>from I-5 south</u>: Exit 169 to 45 st. **R** on 45 st.
　　Curves into Sand Point Way. **L** on 52 to park.

bus: from Downtown, 66 Express. Transfer
　　to bus 75 at Campus Way and Univ. Bay 2.
　　Exit bus 75 at NE 52 St. on Sand Point.

Portage Bay Loop

Distance: 3.2 miles, 60 ft. elevation gain

Start/finish: Montlake Park, 1618 E. Calhoun

From the community center, walk
along park on E. Calhoun.
L onto paved path at end.
Path goes under bridge.
L at street (Montlake Blvd. E.)

2814
Park

UW
fountain

L on E. Hamlin.
R on W. Park Dr. E
R on E. Shelby.

L on Montlak Blvd. E.
Cross Montlake bridge.
Up terrace of steps to UW.
Cross first street (Mason Rd).
L on bike path (Burke-Gilman).

wall of

Under the bridge, by the
"Wall of Death", **R** up steps
to bridge. Cross bridge
on left-hand side.

L at end, on Fuhrman Av. E.
Curves into Boyer. Av. E.
L on E. McGraw St.
L on 18th Av. E to park.

house boats

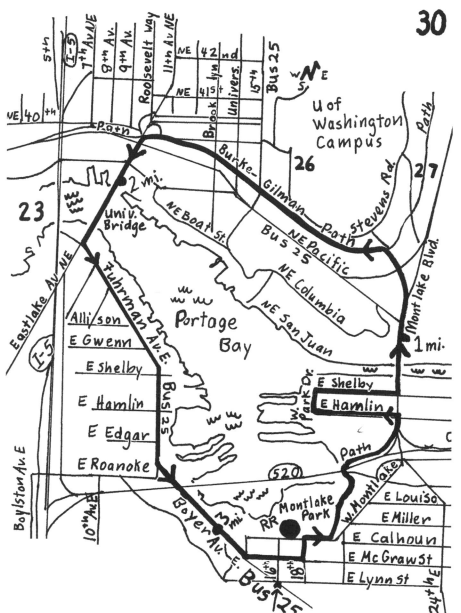

30

Directions to start.

Montlake Community Center. 1618 E. Calhoun St.

car: from I-5 north or south,
Exit 168B (520 bridge).
Take first exit, Montlake Blvd., go R.
R at next light, on Roanoke st. Follow road
At the 5-way stop, sharp R on 16 Av.E.

bus: from Downtown and University, 25.

Montlake to Foster Island

Distance: 2, 3, or 4 miles. Flat.

Start/finish: Montlake Park, 1618 E. Calhoun
At the park, walk along
Calhoun. Straight up hill on path. Camas Paper Mill Mill Stone 1885
L at street (19th).
Curves **R** to Roanoke.
Cross Montlake at light.
R to corner. **L** on Roanoke.
      R into Royal Court, return.
      R on Roanoke.
      L on Lk. Washington Blvd.
      ♦ <u>2 mi. start/finish</u>: in parking
      lot on Lk. Wash. at Miller St.

R on 24th. Over bridge.
R down steps to MOHA.
Between 2 gas lamps, straight
on path to reader board.
Follow path to Foster Island.
      Emerge in parking lot.
      Straight across street.
      Up Arboretum Dr.
      R up steps opposite Visitor Center.
gate at 2457-26E.   Straight on main path.
      Veers **L** to reader board.
      Cross bridge over street.
(**R** for 2 mi. option) (straight for 3 mi. option ✶)
L on 26th. **R** on Boyer, 1 block.
✶**R** on 25th. **L** on Louisa. Cross Louisa St.
 R on Montlake + 24th.
 L on Roanoke.
 R back down path at Calhoun.

Husky Stadium

71

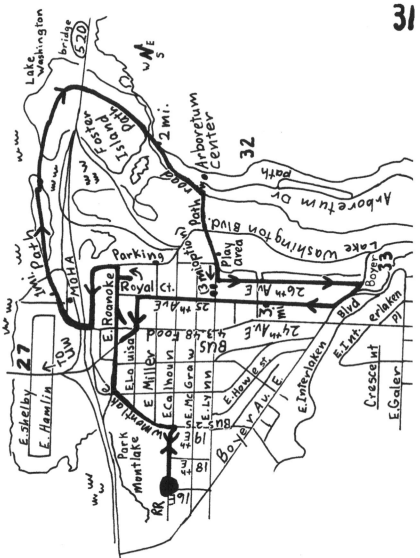

Directions to start.

Montlake Community Center. 1618 E. Calhoun St.

car: from I-5 north or south,
Exit 168B (520 bridge).
Take first exit, Montlake Blvd., go **R**.
R at next light, on Roanoke St. Follow road
At the 5-way stop, sharp **R** on 16 Av. E.

bus: from Downtown and University, 25.

Arboretum

Distance: 1 mi. Walk to "Woodland Garden", return.
2 mi. 60 ft. elevation

Start/finish: Playfield on Lk. Washington Blvd. E at
E. Madison St. Free parking, restrooms.

Walk downhill on Lk. Washington E.
Cross street at first cross walk.
Straight on grassy Azalea Way.
At end of gravel path,
R to Woodland Garden.
R around pond, up small hill.
L at junction, **L** at fork.

L around Winter Garden.
Stay on main path.
L at fork. **R** at next fork,
to Arboretum Center.

R on road (Arboretum Dr.)
At "Magnolia" sign on **R**,
go **L** into small parking lot.
Take path at far end to the
Sorbus Collection. **R** on path.
L on road, where you emerge.

R at big map board, pass it.
L on Main Path.
L up to Pacific Collections.
R down road.
R on busy Lk. Washington Blvd.
Cross carefully to parking lot.

Gazebo

main path

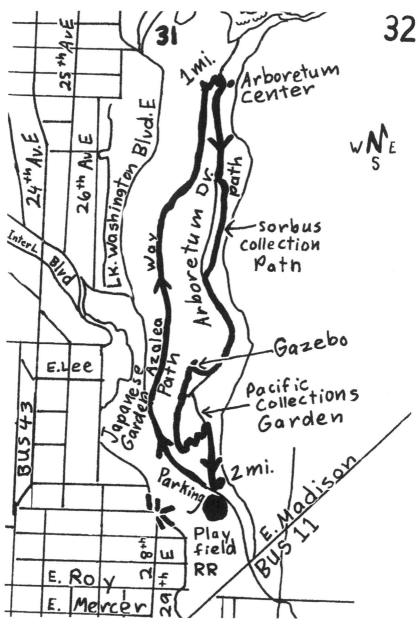

Arboretum Center

1 mi.

W N E S

Sorbus collection Path

Arboretum Dr.

Path

Way

Azalea Path

Japanese Garden

Lk. Washington Blvd. E

25th Av E

24th Av. E

26th Av E

InterL Blvd

Gazebo

Pacific Collections Garden

E. Lee

BUS 43

Parking

2 mi.

E. Madison BUS 11

Play field RR

8th E

2 nd E

E. Roy

E. Mercer

Directions to start.

Washington Park Arobetum Playfield,
on Lake Washington Blvd.E, near Madison st.
car: from I-5 north and south, Exit 168B
to 520 bridge. Take Montlake Blvd.
Exit toward U.W., on to E. Lk. Wash. Blvd.
R on Lk.Wash.Blvd.E. **R** into parking lot.
bus: from Downtown, 11 to Lk.Wash. on Madison.

Above the Arboretum

Distance: 3.3 miles. 184 ft. elevation gain

start/finish: Playfield on Lk. Washington Blu. E at
E. Madison. Free parking, restrooms.

Walk up hill on Lk. Washington Blvd.
R on E. Madison, 1 block.
R on 29th street curves.
At corner, cross to walk on left
side. on sidewalk. At Boyer,
cross to right side, then cross
Boyer, careful! **L** on Boyer.

L on 24th for 2 blocks.
L on Interlaken Pl. E.
NOT before, on Interlaken Blvd.

Veer **R** at Galer, onto 25th Av. E
R at end, (Ward St.) 1 block.
L on 24th Av. E.
L on Thomas, 1 block.
L on E. Madison.

L on Lk. Washington Blvd.

Directions to start.

Washington Park Arobetum Playfield,
on Lake Washington Blvd. E, near Madison st.
car: from I-5 north and south, Exit 168B
to 520 bridge. Take Montlake Blvd.
Exit toward UW., on to E. Lk. Wash. Blvd.
R on Lk. Wash. Blvd. E. **R** into parking lot.
bus: from Downtown, 11 to Lk. Wash. on Madison.

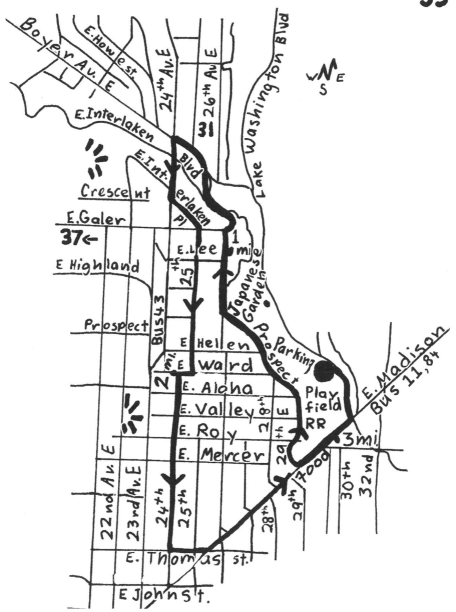

33

Arboretum to Madison Peak

Distance: 1.5 mi. or 3.5 mi. 151 ft. elevation gain.

Start/finish: Playfield on Lk. Washington Blvd. E. at
E. Madison. Free parking. Restrooms.

R up Lk. Washington Blvd. E.
Cross Madison to continue on
Lk. Washington. Cross to left
side of Lk. Washington.

R on 37th (before Hillside st.)
Walk on right side of 37th.
Curves into Dorffel E..
Go straight at Maiden Ln.
Continue on LEFT side of Dorffel.

R up Howell st. R on Madrona Dr.
R through Park shelter, on to
Madrona Place.
L on John. L on 37th.
R on Florence. Sharp right
just before next street,
 (Denny Way).

L on 34th. R on John.
L on 35th to end and return.
Continue down John.
L on 37th. Curves into High st.
L on John, again. L at corner, 37th.
L on Harrison.
R on 30th. R at end. Up stairs.
L on street (Lk. Wash.) back
 to playfield.

P-Patch

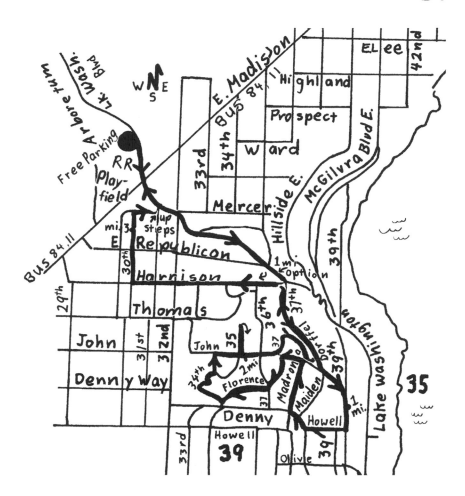

34

Directions to start.

Washington Park Arobetum Playfield,
on Lake Washington Blvd. E, near Madison St.
car: from I-5 north and south, Exit 168B
to 520 bridge. Take Montlake Blvd.
Exit toward U W., on to E. Lk. Wash. Blvd.
R on Lk. Wash. Blvd. E. **R** into parking lot.
bus: from Downtown, 11 to Lk. Wash. on Madison.

Madison Park

Distances: 1 mi. flat, 3.4 mi, 4.5mi, 236 ft. gain

Start/finish: Madison Park, 42nd Av.E.+ E Blaine
   Free 4 hour parking on 42nd. Bus 84,11.
   Restrooms at 43rd and Madison.

R down Madison. **L** on 43rd.
L at end, on McGilvra.
L on 41st. Cross Madison, then
L on Blaine. (1mi. ends here)
   R at end, on 43rd.
   R on Garfield.
   Cross McGilvra, go **L**.
   (for 3.4 mi. **R** on Lk. Wash. Blvd.
   on path. See ■ below.)

Cross Lk. Wash. Blvd. go
straight onto 39th.
At Howell, jog **R** then **L** to
stay on 39th.

   Down steps at end.
   L at the "T" on the bridge.
   straight at the street.
   L at the end, on 40th.

[Washington Pioneer Hall]

R at Olive, down path, then steps.
Cross street (Lk. Wash.) go **L**.
At crosswalk, cross to use left side.
   At 39th, cross Lk. Wash. Blvd.
   ■ to continue uphill on the
   path on right side. Zigzags up
   steeply for one block.
R at street (Hillside), becomes 39th
L up Lee, 1 block. Cross 38th, go **R**.
R on Garfield. **L** on Madison. **R** on 42nd.

250 39th

1622
40th

79

35

Directions to start. *Madison Park*
at E. Madison St. and E. Blaine St.
car: <u>from I-5 north and south</u>: Exit 168 B.
to 520 Hwy. Take Montlake Exit.
onto E. Lake Washington Bld. Curves **R**
onto Lk. Washington Blvd. E.
Through Arboretum. **L** on Madison.
R on Blaine St. to Park.
bus: from Downtown, 11 to Park on Blaine.

Grand Army of the Republic

Distance: 2 mi. or 4 miles. 155 ft. elevation

Start/finish: Volunteer Park at E. Galer + 15th Av. E
Free parking, restrooms in park.

With your back to the Conservatory door,
go straight on to 14th Av. E.

civil War

(for 2 mi. go **R** on Prospect. See ■).
L on E. Roy. Cross 15th, go **R**.
At E. Thomas, cross 15th, and
return down 15th Av.

L on Mercer. **R** on 13th Av. E.
L on Prospect, 1 block. **L** on 12th.
R on Mercer, 1 block. **R** on 11th.
L on Prospect, 1 block.
■ **R** on Federal Way.

814 14Av.E
Moore
Mansion

L on Blaine. Down stairs.
R on Broadway E.
R on Newton.
R on 11th, 1 block.
L on Howe. Explore the Grand
Army of the Republic cemetery.
Continue on Howe.

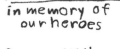

in memory of
our heroes

Cross 15th Av. go **R** 1 short block.
L on Olin, curves through
Boren Park look out.
L on Garfield, 1 short block.
R on Grandview Pl. E.
R on Galer. **L** on 15th Av. to
cross **R** into Volunteer Park
on path.

on 13th

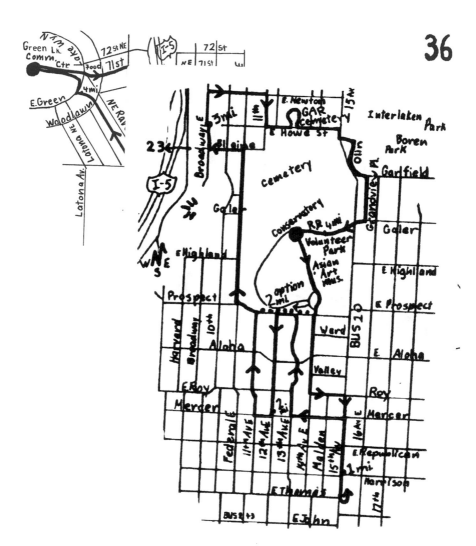

36

Directions to start:

Volunteer Park, 1247 15 Av. E.

car: from I-5 north: Exit 166. **R** on E. Olive Way.
  Merge onto E. John St. **L** on 15 Av. E.
    L in to Volunteer Park.
from I-5 south: Exit 168A. **L** on E. Roanoke St.
  Get in **R** lane. **R** on 10 Av. E.
  L on E. Boston St, turns into 15 Av. E.
    L into Volunteer Park.

bus: from Downtown, 10.

Capitol Hill

Distances: 2.5 or 4 miles. 300 ft. gradual up+down.

Start/finish: Volunteer Park, 15th Av. E + E. Galer
   free parking, restrooms in park.
From the Conservatory, go
downhill. Exit park onto Galer.
R on 16th. **L** on Roy, 1 block.
L on 17th. **R** on Galer, 1 block.
                R on 18th./for 2.5 mi. option,
                            (**R** on Roy. See ■ below.)
                L on Roy. **L** on 20th.
                R on Highland if tired, OR
                       R on Galer 1 block.
R on 21st. **L** on Roy 1 block.
R on 22nd 1 block. **R** on Mercer.
R on 15th, 1 block. **L** on Roy, 1 block.
■ **R** on 14th, in to park.

Asian
Art
museum

Directions to start:
Volunteer Park, 1247 15 Av. E.
car: from I-5 north: Exit 166. **R** on E. Olive Way.
       Merge onto E. John st. **L** on 15 Av. E.
          L in to Volunteer Park.
from I-5 south: Exit 168 A. **L** on E. Roanoke St.
       Get in **R** lane. **R** on 10 Av. E.
       L on E. Boston st, turns into 15 Av. E.
          L into Volunteer Park.
bus: from Downtown, 10.

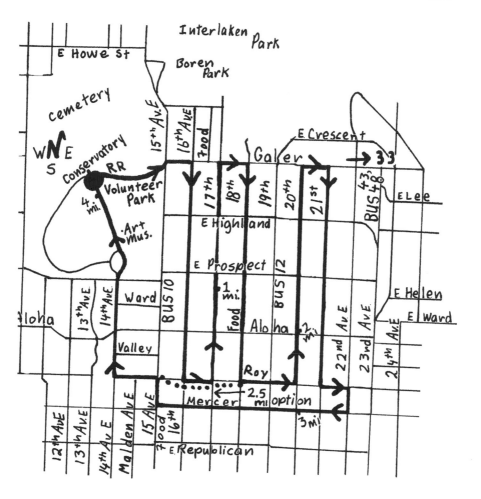

37

Harvard-Belmont Historic Area

Distance: 2.5 mi. or 4 miles. 194 ft. elevation

Start/finish: Volunteer Park, at Galer and 15Av. E
        Free parking, restrooms in park.

With your back to the Conservatory doors,
go straight, on to 14ᵗʰ Av. E.
R on Mercer (for 2.5 mi. go to ■ below) 1 block.

L on 13 Av. E **R** on Olive.
Into Cal Anderson Park.
R on path. **L** around playground
R at old stone building,
along pond. **R** on path to corner.

L on 11ᵗʰ. **L** on Thomas.
Explore P-Patch garden.
■**R** on 10ᵗʰ. **L** on Mercer, 1 Block.
Cross Broadway, go **R**. **L** on Roy.
Curve **R** on downhill.

1051 Summit

R on Summit. **L** around circle.
Curve **R** on Prospect, 1 block.
R on Belmont Place E.
L on Belmont Ave E, 1 block.

1010 Thomas

L on Bolyston. **R** on Prospect, 1 block.
R on Harvard. **L** on Aloha, 1 block.
L on Broadway. **R** on Prospect, 1½ bk.

L on 12ᵗʰ, into park.
Veer **R** to small building.
L on path by this building.

L at round pond, on path.
At next small pond, **R** up steps.
L to Conservatory.

Directions to start on #37

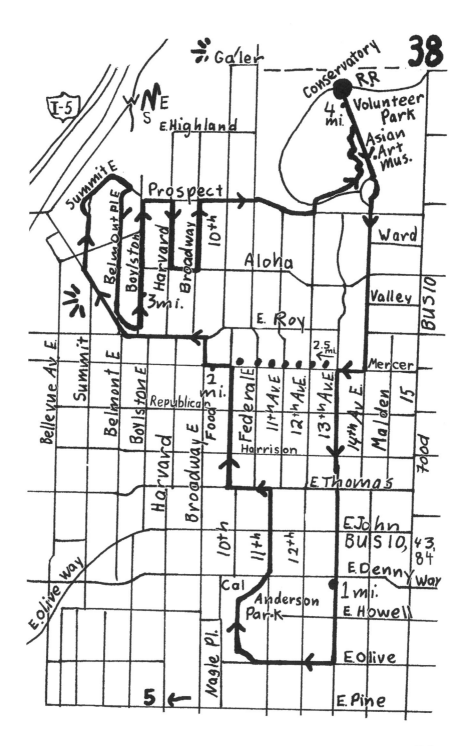

38

Leschi to Madrona

Distance 3.75 miles. Elevation, 295 ft.

Start/finish: Powell Barnett Park at
            E. Jefferson and ML King Jr Way

Walk up hill on Jefferson, 1 block.
R on 29th, 2 blocks.
L on Spruce, one block.
R on 30th, two blocks.

            L on Yesler Way.
            Cross 32nd, go Left.
            Follow down to lake.
            Cross Lk. Washington Blvd.
            L on path. (R to Food!)
            Look R for trail.
            Pass Madrona Beach.

37th &
Pike

L up Madrona Dr. one block.
 (For less steepness, up Madrona,
  Curves to 34th. Rejoin at ✳ below.)
L on Newport Way, one block.
R on Grand, one block.
Curve R on 38th to corner.
L on Pike St. 2 blocks.

on 36th

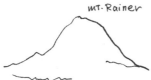

MT. Rainer

            R on 36th, to Schubert, to 35th.
            R on Union, one block.
            L on 34th, 2 blocks.

✳L on Marion, one block.
 R on 35th to end for view,
 Return to James St. Go L.
 L on 32nd one block. R on Jefferson.

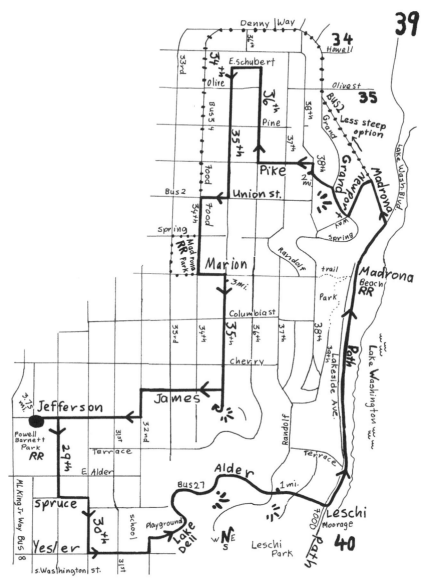

39

Directions to start:

Volunteer Park, 1241 15 Av.E.

car: <u>from I-5 north</u>: Exit 166. **R** on E. Olive Way.
Merge onto E. John st. **L** on 15 Av. E.
  L in to Volunteer Park.

<u>from I-5 south</u>: Exit 168 A. **L** on E. Roanoke St.
Get in **R** lane. **R** on 10 Av. E.
  L on E. Boston st, turns into 15 Av. E.
   L into Volunteer Park.

bus: from Downtown, 10.

Mt. Baker to Leschi

Distance: 2.75 mi. or 5.1 mi. 346 ft. up.
start/finish: Mt. Baker Light Rail or free
          parking on 30th, 31st, nearby.
          <u>Exit</u> Mt. Baker Light Rail,
          Up stairs, over bridge.
          R to cross Mt. Baker, go **R**.

L around high School. **L** on 31st.
Cross boulevard, go **R**, 1 block.
L on 32nd.
L on Plum St. one block.
R on 31st.   (2.75 mi. option - steep downhill -
          At Holgate, **R** down stairs into
          Colman Park. Take paths down
          to lake. **R** along lake. Rejoin at ✪
                                 below)

Cross 31st to enjoy Mt. Baker
Ridge Viewpoint.
R on Day St. which curves to 31st
R on 31st. At Norman St.,
R down path.
L on 32nd, on to path.
          Cross road. Go into Frick Park
          on path. **R** at fork to street.
          Cross 35th. **L** on King to

Cross Lakeside Av. at ped-xing.
R on path along lake.
At Mt. Baker Park, ✪
R on lake side Av. Take the
path to McClellan St.
straight to Mt. Baker Blvd.

89

40

Lake Washington to Puget Sound

Distance: 4 miles or 5.6 miles. 350 ft. elevation
Start: Mt. Baker Light Rail
finish: (4mi.) Intl. Dist Lt. Rail, 5th and Jackson
   (5.6 mi.) Westlake Ctr. Lt. Rail

Exit Mt. Baker Light Rail.
Straight across street, up stairs
over bridge. At end,
R to cross Mt. Baker. R on Mt. Baker.

School
yard art

At end, L around Franklin High
Street curves. Cross McClellan.
Jog L then R down park path.
Cross Lakeside Av. L on path.

Directions to start. Mt. Baker Light Rail.
There is limited parking near the Lightrail.
car: from I-5 north and south: Exit to I-90
   toward Spokane. Get in R lane, fast!
   Exit 3 to Rainer Av. S. L on Mt. Baker Blvd,
   at MLking S. L on 31 Av. S. Free parking
   on street. Join map enroute.
bus: from Downtown, take the Light Rail.
   See Downtown Map for stations.

41

Under ⑨⓪ bridge overpass.
L onto Day St. Jog **R** past bollards.
Uphill on curving path, up steps.
L at top of steps.
R through tunnel, to S. Smith Park.

Atlantic St. Center

cute
house
Award

1143 Sturgus

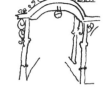

Stay on main path, which curves.
Cross 23rd Av. S. go **L**, then
R down first path. Over bridge,
into Daejeon Park on Sturgus Av. S

R on 12th Av. S. Cross Jackson, go **L**
(4mi. option is Light rail on 5th + Jackson)
R on 1st Av. **L** on Yesler.

Cross Alaskan Way. Go **R**.
R up Pike St. stairs or elevator.
L at street. **R** on Pike.
Cross 4th Av. **L** one block to:
   Westlake Center Light Rail or
   Monorail to Seattle Con. Center

Mt Baker Lt. Rail to Beach

Distance: 2 miles gradual up and down, 180 ft.

Start/finish: Mt. Baker Light Rail.
At beach, free parking, restrooms.
Exit Mt. Baker Light Rail. Cross
street to go up steps. Cross bridge.
At end, **R** to cross S. Mt. Baker Blvd.
R on S. Mt. Baker Blvd.

Curve **L** around high school.
Cross S. McClellan on
crosswalk. Jog **L** then **R**
on path down through park.
Cross Lk. Wash. Blvd. to beach.
Return on path through park.
Straight on to S. Mt. Baker Blvd.
to Light Rail. Use crosswalks!

Directions to start. Mt. Baker Light Rail.
There is limited parking near the Light rail.
car: <u>from I-5 north and south:</u> Exit to I-90
toward Spokane. Get in **R** lane, fast!
Exit 3 to Rainer Av. S. **L** on Mt. Baker Blvd,
at ML king S. **L** on 31 Av. S. Free parking
on street. Join map enroute.
bus: from Downtown, take the Light Rail.
See Downtown Map for stations.

93

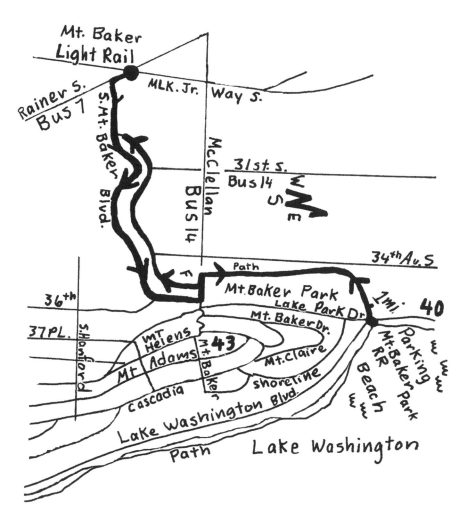

42

Mt. Baker
Light Rail

Rainer S.
Bus 7

MLK. Jr. Way S.

S. Mt. Baker Blvd.

McClellan Bus 14

31st. S.
Bus 14

W N E S

34th Av. S.

36th

Path

Mt. Baker Park

Lake Park Dr.

1 mi.

40

S. Hanford

37 PL.

Mt Helens

Mt. Baker Dr.

Mt Adams

Mt Baker

43

Mt. Claire

Parking Mt. Baker Park RR

Beach

cascadia

shoreline

Lake Washington Blvd.

Path

Lake Washington

Genesse Park to Mt. Baker Park

Distance: 3.4 mi. or 4.4 mi. from Mt. Baker Lt. Rail
 127 ft. elevation

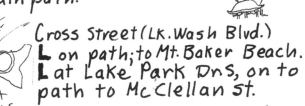

start/finish: Genesse Park HQ at 45th
 OR Mt. Baker Light rail: Exit **L** from Lt. rail steps.
  L to cross street. Up stairs, over bridge.
  R to cross Mt. Baker. Go **R** on Mt. Baker Bld.
  Curve **L** around high school.
  R on McClellan. Join map at ★ below.

At Genesse Park HQ parking lot,
go to the Disabled space.
take the path to the **R**.
L past restrooms. **R** around play area.
Stay on main path.

Cross street (Lk. Wash Blvd.)
L on path; to Mt. Baker Beach.
L at Lake Park Dns, on to
 path to McClellan St.

S Court
42 Av. S

L on McClellan. ★ Straight up path.
L at top, Mt. St. Helens Pl. S.
Curve '**R**' on Cascadia Av. S.

cute house
 a ward

4103 S. Court St.

At S. Ferris St. **L** down Lakewood.
Curve **L** on S. Court St.
R on 42nd Av. S.
L on S. Dakota St. into park.
R on path to parking lot.
(If you took the Mt. Baker
 Lt. Rail, follow directions from
 Genesse Park HQ. above.)

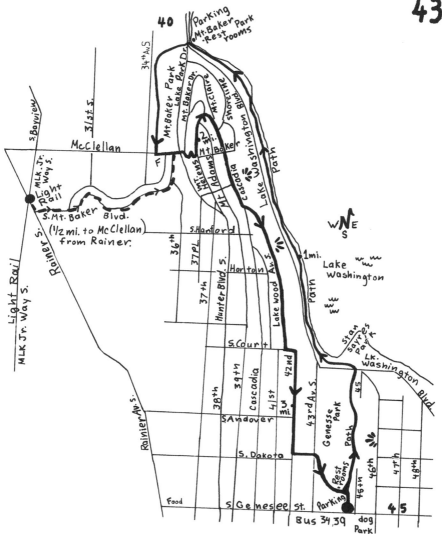

Directions to start. Genesse Park HQ

car: <u>from I-5 north</u>: Exit 3 for Rainer S.
R on Rainer. **L** on S. Genesse.
L into parking lot at park headquarters.
<u>from I-5 south</u>: Exit 161 to Swift Ave.
L on Swift Ave. **R** on Graham.
L on Beacon Av. S. **R** on Columbian Way.
L on Rainer. **R** on S. Genesse.
L into lot at Park headquarters.
bus: from Downtown, 39. Exit at Park HQ.
Light Rail to Mt. Baker. See map for route

Historic Columbia City

Distance: 1 mile. 55 ft. easy elevation gain

Parking: on S. Alaska at 38ᵗʰ Av. S.

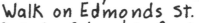

From the Light Rail, exit to
Edmonds. Pick up map with
history at the corner of
Edmonds and MLK Jr Wy S.

Walk on Edmonds St.
L into Columbia Park on
diagonal downhill sidewalk.
R on Rainer Ave. S.
L at S. Hudson to cross street.
L back on Rainer to your start.

There are several restaurants,
shops, a cinema, a theater.
·ColumbiaCity Cinema.com
4816 Rainer, 206·721-3156
·Columbia City Theater.com
4916 Rainer, 206-723-0088
·Genesse Park path starts at
38ᵗʰ and S. Alaska St.

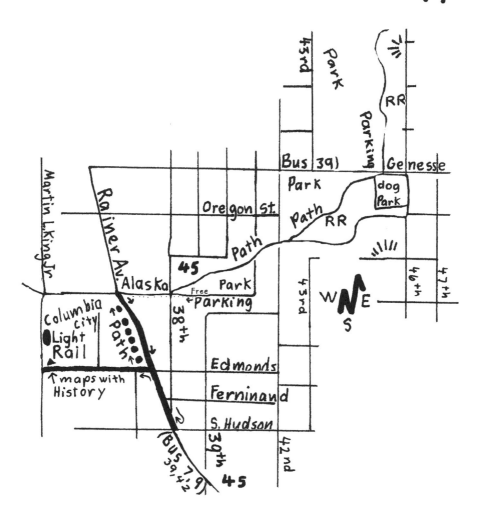

44

Directions to start: Columbia City
Light Rail: Exit to Edmonds, go 2 blocks.
car: from I-5 north and south,
      Exit to Columbia Way. Turns into
      Alaska Way after Rainer. Park after 38st.
bus: from Downtown 7, 9, 39, 42
      from University, 48

Columbia City to Seward Park

Distance: 2.8 mi, 4.5 mi, or 7.5 miles. 144 ft. elevation
From Columbia City Light Rail, add .7 mile.

Start/finish: S. Alaska and Rainer Ave. S.
Free parking on Alaska at 38th by Comm. Center.
From Columbia City Light Rail. Exit to Edmonds.
Free history brochures in Kiosk at Edmonds!
L on Edmonds. **L** down path in park to corner.

seattle PVBlic Library

Walk up Rainer Av. S.
L on Lucille Av.
L on 47th, one block.
R on S. Brandon St.
(2.8 mile option: **L** on Wilson, 50th.
(**L** on Genesse. Rejoin at✱ below)
(**L** on 46th.)

L on 54th, 2 blocks. **R** on Dawson.
L on Orcas. Cross Lk. Wash. Blvd.
(7.5 mi. option. Go into Seward Park.
  R on path, returning to entry.
  R on path along Lk. Wash. Blvd.
(4.5 mi. **L** on path along lake.)

L at Mt. Baker Rowing Center to
cross street (Lk. Wash. Blvd.)
Enter park on path. **L** at fork.
Stay on main path. **L** around
playground, past parking lot.
Cross Genesse St., go **L**.
✱**R** on 46th along dog park.
R on path above soccer field.
L at fork. Cross street (42nd).
L at next fork in path, around
playground to Alaska St.
Straight on Alaska to Rainer.

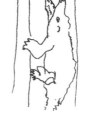

45

Directions to start: Columbia City
Light Rail: Exit to Edmonds, go 2 blocks.
car: from I-5 north and south,
Exit to Columbia Way. Turns into
Alaska Way after Rainer. Park after 38st.
bus: from Downtown 7, 9, 39, 42
from University, 48

Beacon Hill

Distance: 2.5 mi. or 4.7 mi. 120 ft. elevation

Start/finish: Beacon Hill Light Rail at
Beacon Av. S. and S. Lander St.
free parking enroute at 13th Av. S
and McCllelan. Walk on McCllelan
to Beacon. **R** on Beacon. See **∗** below.

Exit Light Rail. **L** on Beacon Av.
∗ L on Forest, 1 Block. **R** on 18 Av, 1 BK.
L on Stevens, 1 BK. **R** on 19th.
R on Hinds, 1 Bk.
Cross 18 Av, go **L** 1 block.
R on Spokane, 1 Block.
Cross Beacon Av., go **L**.
R in to Jefferson Park to explore.
Return to Beacon Av., go **R** to
Community Ctr. Then return on Beacon.

L on Hinds St. Jog **R** on 14 Av. S.
L on Horton. Curves **R** on 13 Av. S.
L on to Hanford. **R** on 12 Av. S.
R on McClellan, 1 block.
(for 2.5 mi., straight on McClellan.
(**L** on Beacon to Light Rail.)

East
is
West

L on 13 Av, 1 BK. **R** on Lander, 1 Block.
L on 14 Av, **L** on Walker, 1 Block.
R on 13th Av. S.

L on Judkins st, 1 block.
Cross 12 Av, go **R**, to Rizal Park.
At Jose Rizal Park SIGN, use
crosswalk to cross 12 Av., into
courtyard to flag, to street.
R on 14 Av.
L on Hill. st. **R** on 16 Av.

46

Directions to start:
Car: From I-5 north, Exit 163A:
from I-5 South, Exit 163:
from I-90, take I-5 South, Exit 163A:
To Columbia Way. **L** on 15th. **L** on McClellan
to free parking past 13th. Walk on
McClellan. **L** on Beacon to Light Rail-Start.
Bus: from downtown, 36 to Rainer Beach.
Light Rail: Beacon Hill.

Chief Sealth Trail A

Othello Light Rail Station to Dawson St.

Distance: 1.5 mi. 135 ft. gain. 2.5 mi. 165 ft. gain
4 mi. 203 ft. elevation gain

Start/finish: Othello Light Rail Station.
Free parking on 37Av.S. or 38A
No public rest rooms.

view of Olympic mtns.

From the Othello Light Rail,
exit to Myrtle St. Pass King Plaza.
L on Myrtle St. to end.
L on path in J. Little Park.
R at street (Myrtle PL) ½ block.
R up path, Chief Sealth Trail.

L on the first street (Holly Pk. Dr
(or return the way you came
(for 1.5 mi. walk.)
R up 32 Av.S. to curve to go
L on S. Holly St.

At Beacon St., cross to path
in middle of boulevard.
R on path.
(for 2.5 mi. R on Morgan St.
(to trail. R down trail, back
(through park to Light Rail.)

Mt. Rainer

R on Dawson St. to Chief Sealth
Trail. R down trail, Return
through park to Light Rail.

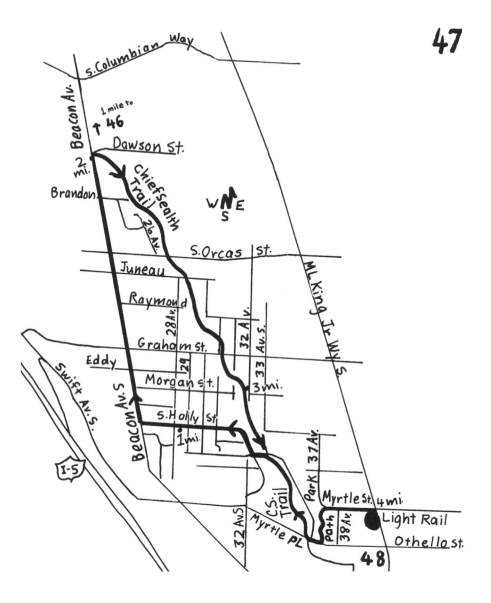

Directions to start: Othello Light Rail
ML King Jr. Way S. at S. Myrtle.
car: <u>from I-5 north</u>: Exit 161. **L** on S. Albro.
   R on Swift Av. S., curves on to S. Myrtle.
   L on 39 Av. S. Free parking on street.
<u>from I-5 south</u>: Exit 157 on to ML King S.
   L on S. Myrtle to park. Free parking.
Light Rail: comes from Downtown.

Chief Sealth Trail B
Othello Light Rail to Rainer Beach Light Rail

Distance: 1.5 mi. flat, or 1.5 mi. 123 ft. elevation
2.8 mi. 246 ft. elevation

Start/finish: Othello Light Rail. Free parking on
38 Av. S. No restrooms.

Exit Othello Light Rail to Myrtle St.
L on Myrtle to J. Little Park.
L on path through the park.
Cross the street (S. Myrtle Pl.)
Jog **L** then **R** on Holly Park. Dr.
Follow signs to Chief Sealth Trail.
Curve **L**, then **R** on 39 Av. S.

(for 1.5 mi. flat, **L** on Kenyon St.
(Rejoin at * below.
At the big uphill curve,
straight onto the trail.
At Rainer Beach Light Rail
return to Kenyon St. or on
Light Rail to Othello for 1.5 mi. walk

R on Kenyon St. one block.
L on ML King Wy. S.
L on Chicago St. one block.
R on Iago St. Take path
through park to playfield.
Continue along right side of
40 Av. S.

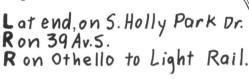

L at end, on S. Holly Park Dr.
R on 39 Av. S.
R on Othello to Light Rail.

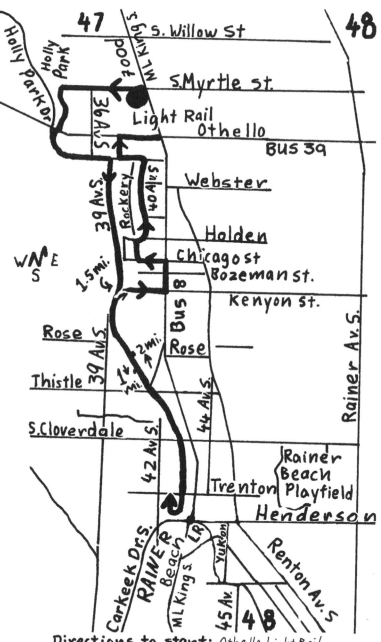

Holly Park Dr.

Holly Park

S. Willow St

7000

ML King S.

S. Myrtle St.

39 Av S.

Light Rail

Othello

Bus 39

Rockery

40 Av S.

39 Av. S.

Webster

Holden

Chicago St

Bozeman St.

Kenyon St.

W N E
S

1.5 mi.

Bus 8

Rose S.

Rose

2 mi.

39 Av. S.

1½ mi.

Thistle

44 Av S.

S. Cloverdale

42 Av. S.

Rainer
Beach
Playfield

Trenton

Henderson

Rainer Av. S.

Carkeek Dr. S.

RAINER

Beach

ML King S.

LR

Yukon

45 Av.

Renton Av. S.

48

Directions to start: Othello Light Rail
ML King Jr. Way S. at S. Myrtle.
car: <u>from I-5 north</u>: Exit 161. **L** on S. Albro.
    R on Swift Av. S., curves on to S. Myrtle.
    L on 39 Av. S. Free parking on street.
<u>from I-5 south</u>: Exit 157 onto ML King S.
    L on S. Myrtle to park. Free parking.
Light Rail: comes from Downtown.

Chief Sealth Trail C
Rainer Beach Light Rail to Kubota Garden

Distance: ½ mi. around Kubota Garden.

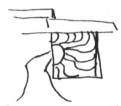
Free parking at Kubota Garden.
Restroom at Garden.
2.4 mi. 111 ft. - Follow Renton Av. s.
2.7 mi. 157 ft. - steep at first.

From Rainer Beach Light Rail,
exit to Henderson St.
Go downhill ½ block.
R on Chief Sealth Trail.
At 48 Av. and Roxbury st.,
stay on Roxbury St.
Cross 51Av. **R** on Renton Av.S.

R on 55 Av. into Kubota Garden.
Pick up a brochure, or
Wander **R** through Garden.
Find the Historical Garden.

Return on Chief Sealth Trail,
or easier way on Renton Av. S
L on Henderson St.

KUBOTA
GARDEN

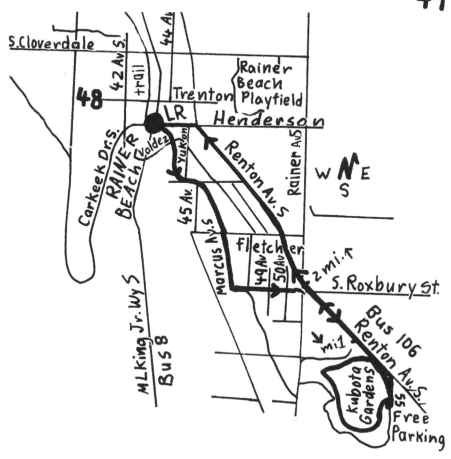

49

Directions to start: Rainer Beach Light Rail
car: Free parking at Kubota Garden on
    55 St. S. at Renton Av. S.
from I-5 north: Exit 158. **L** at end.
    Becomes S. Ryan Way, **R** on S. 107 St.
    Becomes S. Creston St. **L** on 55 Av. S.
from I-5 south: Exit 157 on to ML King S.
    R on S. Ryan Way. **R** on S. 107 St.
    Becomes S. Creston. **L** on 55 Av. S.
Light Rail: Comes from Downtown.   108

West Seattle Beach

Distance: 1 mi. to big curve to left and back.

4 mi. to 57 Av. and back.
7.5 mi. to Me Kwa Mooks Park and back
13.6 mi. to end of Lincoln Park and back
All flat shoreline.

Start/finish: Seacrest Park - water taxi dock.
Water taxi runs seasonaly
from Seattle Pier 52.
Restrooms. Free parking
along Alki Beach.

From Seacrest Park, exit lot,
R along shore on sidewalk.
At 57 Av. opposite restrooms, go
L on 57 Av. one block.
R on Lander, two blocks.
R on 59 Av.
L on Alki Av. along beach.
At end of trail, continue on
sidewalk.

Carrol street history marker

playground

L at sw Oregon st. into
Me Kwa Mook's Park to
history plaque.
Return on Beach Dr.

R on 64 Av.   **R** on Alki Av. sw

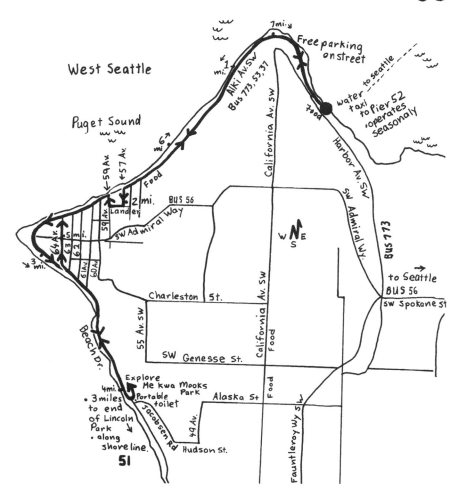

50

West Seattle

Puget Sound

7 mi. ↘

Free parking on street

water to seattle

water taxi to Pier 52 operates seasonaly

Alki Av. SW
Bus 773, 53, 37

↙ 1 mi.

California Av. SW

Food

Harbor Av. SW

SW Admiral Wy.

↖ 6 mi.

59 Av.
←57 Av.

Food

↙ 2 mi.
Landey
BUS 56

59 Av.

64 Av.
63
62
61
60 Ave.

↙ 5 mi.

SW Admiral Way

W N E S

to Seattle
BUS 56

SW Spokane St

↙ 3 mi.

BUS 773

Charleston St.

55 Av. SW

California Av. SW

Food

Beach Dr.

SW Genesse St.

Explore Me kwa Mooks Park

4 mi.
• 3 miles to end of Lincoln Park
• along shoreline.

Portable toilet

Jacobsen Rd

49 Av.

Alaska St

Food

Fauntleroy Wy SW

Hudson St.

51

Directions to start. Seacrest Park or anywhere along Harbor Av. sw.
car: from I-5 north: Exit 163.
from I-5 south: Exit 163A.
Cross West Seattle Bridge. Exit to Harbor Av.
R into Seacrest lot, or continue down street for more **than 2** hours free parking.

Lincoln Park to Downtown
west seattle

Distance: 1 to 6mi. flat beach walk.

2 mi. Top of hill. Start/finish at Park
on 48 Av. and Oregon. Up on 48 Av.
R on Oregon. L on 46 Av.
R on Spokane. R on 44 Av.
L on Dakota, R on Calif. R on Alaska.

7 mi. 341 ft. or 8.6 mi, 383 ft. up.

Start/finish: Lincoln Park at Fauntleroy + Cloverdale
Free parking. Restrooms on beach.
For flat walks. walk down past info.
board. It is 1 mi. to end of park,
3 miles to kwa Mooks Park.

Walk up hill to end of parking lot.
Take trail veering L toward beach.
Cross a creek. Past a playground.
A rail fence is on your left.
At end, exit R to street.
Continue straight, on Fontonelle.
L on fauntleray Wy., curves.

L on 41 Av. L on Findlay, 1 block.
R on 42 Av. L on Edmunds, 1 block.
R on California Av.
(for 7mi. L on Alaska. Rejoin at ✱)
L on Dakota, 1 block. R on 44 Av.
L on Spokane. L on 46 Av.

R on Oregon.
R on Alaska. ✱ L on 50 Av.
R on Hudson, curves to Jacobsen.
Cross Beach Dr. go L to end.
L up driveway to parking lot.

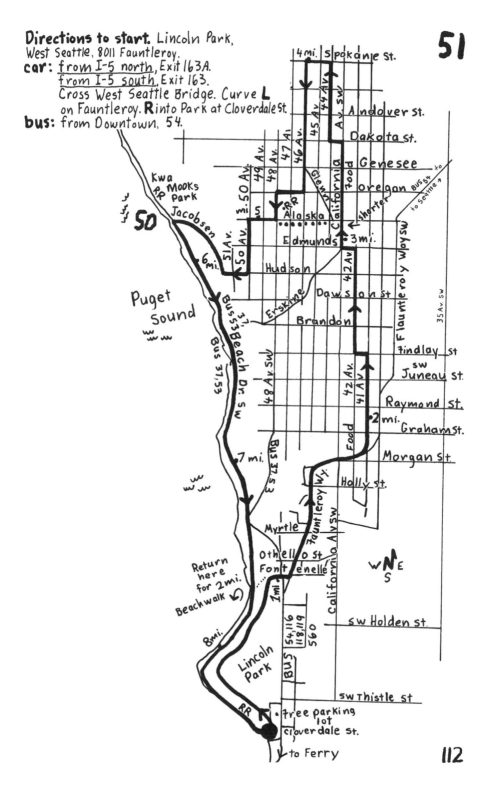

Bainbridge Ferry

Distance: 1.2 mi. easy, 3 mi. 137 ft., or 4.1 mi. 210 ft.

Start/finish: Bainbridge Ferry Terminal

Walk from the Ferry to the traffic
light. **L** (toward Eagle Harbor Condos.)
R on Waterfront Trail.
L at fork, to trail along the shore.
R at dock. **L** at restrooms.
Curve into Shannon Way.
L on Bjune. **R** on Madison, 1 block.

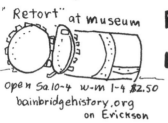

"Retort" at museum

open Sa.10-4 w-m 1-4 $2.50
bainbridgehistory.org
on Erickson

R on Winslow Way, one block.
 (for 1.2 mi., continue to Ferry)
L up Erickson, on left side.
 (for 3 mi., **L** on Wyatt Way,
 L on Cosgrove. Rejoin at ✳.)

At end of Erickson St. continue
on path at right, onto Hildebrand.
L at end, High School Road.
(Best Western Bainbridge hotel is here.)

FAO Schwartz
Bear

Richie's 305 Madison

Classic 1948 Diner

L down Weaver Rd.
Cross Wyatt Way, one block.
R on Cosgrove. ✳ **L** at end.
L at next deadend, up trail.
Only the first 50 paces are steep

R at end, on Madison.
L on Winslow Way, to Ferry.

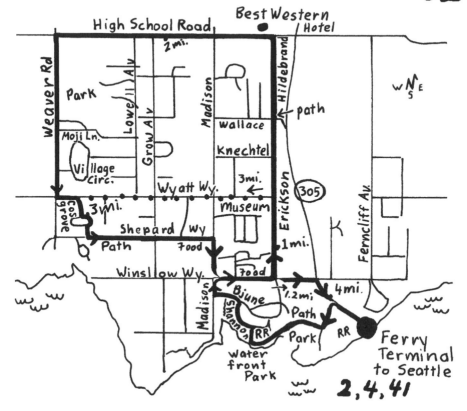

Directions to start. Ferry Terminal.
On Alaskan Way at Yesler Way.
car: from I-5 north: Exit 165B to Union St.
L on 5 Av. **R** on Madison St. **L** on Alaskan Wy.
from I-5 south: Exit 164A to Madison St.
L on Madison St. **L** on Alaskan Way.
light rail: Pioneer Square Station
Walk down hill on James St.
R on 1 Av. **L** on Marion St.

Diary of a Walker

Route	Miles - Date	Notes

Diary of a Walker

Route	Miles· Date	Notes

Diary of a Walker

Route	Miles-Date	Notes

Diary of a Walker

Route	Miles· Date	Notes

Diary of a Walker

Route	Miles - Date	Notes

Diary of a Walker

Route	Miles · Date	Notes

Diary of a Walker

Route	Miles · Date	Notes

Diary of a Walker

Route	Miles · Date	Notes

About the Author
and Illustrator, Tyler E. Burgess

Born in 1950 in the shadow of the Bighorn mountains, I grew up on a cattle ranch near Sheridan, Wyoming. While earning a Business degree at the University of Wyoming, I married, had two children, Sara and Damon. We moved to Billings, Montana, raised the children, divorced and eventually I moved to Eugene, Oregon, where my son was a student.

For athletics, I have always loved outdoor sports. In my 40's I played soccer, did triathlons, multi-sport events, solo backpack trips.

In 2000 I founded Walk With Me, and have coached marathon walking training, taught fitness walking classes at the University of Oregon and Lane Community College.

Also I have organized and led walking trips across England, in Ireland, Italy and Morocco. Plus New York City, Boston and Washington DC.

In the fall of 2008 I did a solo walk 550 miles in Spain, the pilgrimage, Way of St. James.

Other Books:
Walking Made Powerful
Eugene, Oregon Walks
Oregon Townscape Walks